MIDNIGHT

"And at midnight Paul and Silas prayed, and sang praises unto God: and the prisoners heard them."
— Acts 16:25

FIDEL M. DONALDSON

This book is dedicated to King Jesus: He made the darkness light for me

Midnight by Fidel M. Donaldson
Copyright © 2010 Appeal Ministries

ISBN: 978-09827710-1-3
LCCN: 010907253

Cover design by: Integrative Ink

Printed in the United States of America

TABLE OF CONTENTS

FOREWORD

In Scriptures, the term midnight is a very important principle. What we do at midnight, the darkest hour of the day, will determine many things related to our walk with God. Midnight is a time of darkness, testing, and trial. It is a time of great judgment, as well as an important principle in relation to the bride of Christ, or church described in Ephesians 5:25-27. The bible gives examples of several people enduring during midnight trials. You may relate to Israel experiencing the "Passover" at midnight as God's judgment was carried out, or Paul and Silas who began to praise and thank God in their deep trial of faith at midnight while chained in stocks in an inner prison. You may even be like the ten virgins hearing the call of the bride of God at midnight. Whoever we are, we learn that what we do at midnight determines a lot about our walk with God.

My precious friend and minister Fidel Donaldson knows quite a bit about this principle. He has been through many midnight experiences and has overcome, which makes him qualified to write this book. You can not give something you do not have. He has heard the "call of the bride" and is actively running the race to obtain bride-ship. He is also a true worshipper and has seen God deliver him from his midnight testings. You could almost say his life has been one of many "midnight experiences" which has made him the man of God he is today. This enables him to give us true revelation from the Word, as well as from his own life experiences.

In this tremendous book you will find revelation out of the Scriptures to determine the decisions you make in the midnight hour. You will also find great encouragement about our calling to be Jesus' holy bride and how to respond to that call. All of us have midnight experiences, and it is essential that we know what to do in that trying time. This book will help you to know what is happening and why, and it will teach you how to respond in that hour.

I believe we are living in the last days, and surely the Bridegroom is calling us to Himself at this midnight hour. It is vital to know what to do and how to overcome these situations. This book will enlighten, encourage, and teach you all you need to know as we, the body of Christ, go through this midnight hour. However, we will overcome, and take our rightful place as His bride. When you have finished reading this book, you will praise and thank God for Reverend Donaldson's tremendous insight into this principle. As for me, I will respond like King David, *"At midnight I will rise to give thanks unto thee"* (Psalms 119:62)! Thanks Brother Fidel for writing this timely and proceeding word from our glorious Lord Jesus!

AUTHOR'S NOTE

We are on the cusp of the dawning of a new day, and with it will come a greater manifestation of the Glory of God. Before we experience the new day we will have to get through midnight. Midnight represents a season of gross darkness, but it also represents the earliest point of the new day. This season of darkness will represent a time of spiritual and moral decline such as the earth has never experienced.

As believers we have to be at the highest level of consecration and sanctification because people will be looking for a way out of the darkness. God has placed us in the earth to be His light shining in a dark place and midnight will give us the opportunity for sinners to see the light of Jesus shining in and through us. Spiritual darkness will cover the earth in the manner in which the natural darkness covered the earth at the time of creation. The light of the glorious gospel of the Lord Jesus in us will counteract the darkness of midnight but we have to continue to die to the flesh so God the Holy Spirit can continue to shine His light through us. As you read this book my hope and prayer is that it will encourage you to draw closer to Jesus so He can prepare you for the coming of midnight.

Chapter 1
MIDNIGHT

Death, chaos and demonic activity take place at midnight, according to polish author Peter Kowalski. In his book *Lexicon Signs of The World -- Omen Superstition*, Kowalski described the meaning of midnight from a cultural perspective. The author stated that traditional magical thinking alludes to the term midnight as being solar midnight, or the opposite of solar noon. It is the apogee of darkness and perigee of light, creating an axis that connects to other worlds.

Kowalski stated that midnight is a supernatural hour, complete with ghosts rising from the grave and demonic possessions. Acts of witchcraft and sorcery were performed at this hour, including harvesting herbs at their highest point of potency for ritualistic use. The literary work states that midnight also symbolizes the end of the world according to the the modern world Doomsday Clock.

The term midnight is unique in that it marks the beginning and ending of each day in the civil world. In *The Call of the Bride*, published by Glory Publishing, Dr. Samuel Greene spoke about the hour from a biblical perspective. *"Midnight in the scriptures speaks of great darkness. It is the height of warfare, the darkest hour of the day, the toughest part of our warfare."* There are various Hebrew translations for the term midnight. In Hebrew, the term means the middle of the night, to split into or to divide, to halve, to reach to the midst, or to live out half. Midnight is the apex of darkness. Midnight also means to sever in Hebrew.

Although midnight marks the dawning of a new day, it is difficult to discern its newness. When the hands of the clock strike 12 a.m., it looks just as dark outside as it did the previous hour. The new day actually begins in darkness. Chronologically, the day may have changed but the conditions look the same on the outside. Spiritually speaking, this is important to note because the darkness of a situation might lead you to believe nothing has changed. But you must remember, although you cannot see the newness of the day, it is a new day sixty seconds after 11:59 pm. If you can hold on and keep your faith, eventually you will see the darkness give way and the light of the sun begin to shine. The outward appearance of a situation may be akin to the look of midnight in that it is still dark outside when the new day arrives. However we must not go by what we see. We must go by what we know.

No matter how dark or bleak it looks on the outside, we must take comfort in the fact that a new day has dawned, and with it comes another opportunity to walk in the light. The Psalmist David declared, *"Weeping may endure for a night but joy cometh in the morning" (Psalm 30:5b).* Joy comes in the morning because light comes in the morning and we are able to see and discern things we could not discern in the night season. The challenge for each of us is to be able to endure the uncertainty of our night seasons. There are varying degrees of trials and testing in the night seasons of our lives. Midnight represents the darkest, the most severe trials we have to face. It is under the cover of night that many dark deeds are done, so we have to walk circumspect and guard ourselves against the attacks and temptations that accompany the night. It was at night that Lot's daughters made him drink wine so they could lay down with him. It was in the night when God came to Abimelech in a dream and told him he was a dead man because he had taken Sarai, Abram's wife.

Some seasons are darker than others but no matter how dark the season or hour, God has sufficient light to deal with it. The testing and the trials we endure in the night seasons of our lives give us a greater appreciation for the morning. The morning speaks of a time of deliverance, a time when the darkness is replaced by light. Job declared, *"When I lie down, I say, when shall I arise, and the night be gone? And I am full of tossing to and fro unto the dawning of the day" (Job 7:4).* It is in the night season of our trials where a spirit of heaviness will attempt to overtake us. We must find a way to put on the garment of praise. The enemy will have room to operate if we allow ourselves to sink into a pit of despair. There are certain night seasons that are so long, they appear as if they are not going to pass. In those seasons we must continue to walk by faith, keep trusting in the Lord, and know that the morning is coming.

There is something eerily mysterious about the night. As a child I remember how terrified I was when I had to go down to the basement at night time. I tried to find the light switch as quickly as possible. I am sure most of the terror was a figment of my imagination and the fact that I could not see in the dark. When the eye cannot see what is around it, the mind will conjure up all kinds of thoughts and images. There are times as an adult when I am home alone and there are certain noises that I can hear in the house at night. In those instances, it is easy to become fearful of the unknown, but I do not allow a spirit of fear to overtake me. I simply pray and take authority over any and everything that is trespassing in the night. God rules the day and the night so we do not have to worry when we are in the night season. One of the greatest weapons Satan uses against the believer is fear, because it cripples and paralyzes the believer. Far too many people are not able to rest at night because they are tormented. They stay up all night agonizing over the issues of life instead of placing them in the hands of the Lord and allowing Him to give them sweet sleep. Many of them have to load up on medication just to sleep.

When we place our issues in the hands of Jesus, He will not only give us peace in the night, but He will give us songs in the night. David declared, *"I will both lay me down in peace, and sleep: for thou, LORD only makest me dwell in safety" (Psalm 4:8)*. We can rest in the night seasons of our lives and have peace, because God is up and He is watching over us. Since God is awake and He has the situation under control, why should we be tormented with fear and anxiety? *"Behold, he that keepeth Israel shall neither slumber nor sleep. The LORD is thy keeper: the LORD is thy shade upon thy right hand. The sun shall not smite thee by day, nor the moon by night. The LORD shall preserve thee from all evil: he shall preserve thy soul" (Psalm 121:5-7)*. In Jesus Christ we have protection from all evil. The only way the enemy can gain an opening against us in the midnight hour is if we let him through fear and doubt. When David said, "He shall preserve thy soul," he used the Hebrew word for preserve, *shamar*. It means, *"to hedge about (as with thorns), to guard, to protect."*

The soul is the seat of man's intellect, his will, and his emotions. It is in this arena that the enemy wages war against the believer, and midnight is when he launches his greatest attacks. Through prayer, praise, and the meditation on God's word, our minds will be hedged about, guarded, and protected. When the Lord places a hedge around our minds the enemy will not be able to cause a breach. As long as we keep our minds on Jesus, we will prevail. The enemy will use battering rams such as doubt, unbelief, fear, depression, and anxiety to wear down our mental defense. We have to use our offensive weapons against him and his minions. Remember what the Apostle Paul said, *"For the weapons of our warfare are not carnal, but mighty through God to the pulling down of strongholds; casting down imagination, and every high thing that exalteth itself against the knowledge of God, and bringing into captivity every thought to the obedience of Christ" (2 Corinthians 10:4-5).* A stronghold is like a fortified castle erected by the enemy. God has given us weapons to tear down every stronghold erected by the enemy. Paul understood that the mind of a believer is the place where the enemy tries to erect his strongholds or fortresses. For this reason, he instructs the believer, to cast down imaginations, cast down high things which try to exalt themselves against the knowledge of God, and bring into captivity every thought to the obedience of Christ. Our minds can conjure up some evil thoughts so it may seem like an uphill battle to take every thought captive. It is difficult to overcome this, but it is not impossible. Our minds have been conditioned to think a certain way because of the type of images we have allowed into it. When we allow thoughts of lust and perversion to permeate our thoughts for years, a stronghold is developed. We have to make a concerted effort to store up the word of God in our minds. We must meditate on the scriptures and the goodness of the Lord. Eventually the wicked thoughts will be driven out. The devil knows that the mind is the battleground of spiritual warfare. He knows that thought precedes action, so by controlling our thoughts he will be able to control our minds.

When the devil attempts to erect strongholds of lascivious thoughts in our minds through perversion, we have to cast them down immediately. We must not allow those thoughts to remain until they conjure up images or mental pictures. The moment they come into our heads, we must get rid of them. The desire to sin usually begins with a thought or some form of enticement from the devil. The Apostle James declared, *"But every man is tempted, when he is drawn away (by) his own lust, and enticed. Then when lust hath conceived, it bringeth forth sin: and sin, when it is finished, bringeth forth death" (James 1:14-15).* The devil's ultimate goal is to kill us. His plan is to plant a seed of enticement in our minds. He does this by using something that causes weakness in our flesh. Once the seed is planted and conception takes place, he entices us to act upon our sinful thoughts, hoping our actions will produce death.

We must not give the devil any room in our minds to operate. When he comes against our minds, he must encounter a sign that reads, **"No vacancy."**

Jesus has equipped us with what we need to survive the attacks coming in the night season. We have the word and we have the indwelling of the Holy Ghost. When we are feeling pressed in the midnight hour we must stand in the power of the Holy Ghost and speak the word of the Lord. The darkness might not move right away, but the Holy Ghost and the word will comfort and fortify us until light begins to shine in our situation. Looking back over my life I do not know how I survived the crisis I faced when I did not have a relationship with the Lord, when I did not have the baptism of the Holy Ghost, and when the word of God did not have preeminence in my life. I used alcohol, illicit sex and other things to appease the carnal nature. Despite appeasing my carnal nature, doing these things gave me no lasting comfort. All they did was open the door for more ungodly behavior. All I can say is "thank God" for His grace and His mercy, because they kept me even when I was in rebellion against Him. What a mighty, gracious, and loving God we serve.

MY MIDNIGHT: A PERSONAL TESTIMONY

Every one of us will face a midnight crisis at some point in our lives. The adversity of midnight will either give us strength and build character or it will cause us to become fearful and indecisive. Many years ago I heard someone say, "Once bitten twice shy." Midnight can come upon us because of bad decisions we make, or it can come from something out of our control, like a diagnosis of cancer, heart disease or some other news that strikes panic and fear in us. Whether it comes from a self inflicted wound or something we had no control over, we must trust the Lord to bring deliverance in the midnight hour. Our posture and disposition at midnight can determine the duration and the outcome of the crisis. If a person gets news that there are radical cancer cells growing in his body, the diagnosis can cause their mind to reel with fear and anxiety, especially if the prognosis is unfavorable. Fear can cause a person to give up instead of fight. Panic can also cause a great deal of mental stress which can exacerbate further physical ailments. In the midnight crisis the challenge will be to keep the mind strong; keep the mind from sinking into a pit of despair. It is not easy to fight the encroachment of fear and anxiety when an evil report is received. Do not try to fight the battle alone, know that the Lord is with you and He will see you through.

In the midnight hour the enemy will use sadness, depression, and despair to drive us into a lonely place. He wants us to sit in the dark by ourselves so that he can wreak havoc on our minds. He wants us to shut out others so the only voice we will hear is his. In times of midnight crisis, we have to come out of the dark place of despair. We must not allow the devil to separate and isolate us from the people who love us. The devil will deceive us into believing no one cares about what we are going through. When we feel as if the people around us are not sensitive to the things we are dealing with, we must have faith in God, and know that He cares for us.

In November 1990, I made a decision that plunged me into one of the darkest seasons of my life. Ironically, it was also the season that changed my life for the better. It caused me to take a good look at the life I had lived up to that point. I must tell you that I was not pleased with what I saw. Your darkest hour can be your brightest hour if you are willing to take an honest assessment of the situation and not seek playing the "blame game."

I was arrested in England and charged with conspiracy to smuggle cocaine into the country. While I was on remand I found out that some of my former associates were arrested in the United States and were exchanging information for less prison time. There is a midnight situation we will face in this life that can overwhelm us and bring a sense of fear and anxiety upon us. I was on remand for twenty three hours a day for a couple of months. I could not see much light, because I was facing a lengthy prison sentence in England and in the United States. The midnight crisis forced me to be very introspective. Normally, we do not take a good look at our lives when things are going well. Some people decide to quit smoking when they receive news that they have heart disease or lung cancer, some stop abusing alcohol when they receive news that they have cirrhosis of the liver, some stop being promiscuous when they receive news that they have been infected with the HIV Virus.

The dungeon like conditions of Wormwood Scrubs and Brixton Prison in England forced me to look at the choices I had made in life which led me to those dark places. It did not take long for me to realize that an ungodly lifestyle and a desire to please and appease my flesh were the things that caused midnight to overtake me. The works of the flesh brought me to that dark point in my life, and a decision had to be made if my mind was to be set free. As terrible as my environment was on remand, I knew that it was important for my mind to be set free from the power of sin infecting my body. If authorities had let me out the day after I was arrested and my mind was not changed, I would have went right back to the lifestyle that led me to the prison in the first place. *"As a dog returneth to his vomit, so a fool returneth to his folly" (Proverbs 26:11).* The fool is the person who continues in his folly, oblivious of the destruction that lies ahead.

Bob Marley once said, *"Every day you carry your bucket to the well, one day the bottom will fall out."* I believe it was Marcus Garvey who said, *"A man does not know himself until his back is against the wall."* Someone once described insanity as, *"doing the same things every day but expecting different results."* I ignored repeated warnings about my destructive behavior, because I was caught up in a lifestyle that was pleasing to my flesh.

When the bottom fell out I realized that I had gotten myself into a situation that could be very detrimental if I did not receive mercy. The one whom I needed mercy from was God. I had no relationship with Him, because I repeatedly rejected the word of warning He sent me on many occasions. I am glad He is not like men. I am glad He is long suffering, full of mercy and grace. It is better to repent quickly because we will suffer long if we fail to do so. No matter how terrible your life is, He will answer you if you call on Him from a place of repentance. Remand gave me the opportunity to take an honest assessment of the kind of husband and father I was. I must be honest; I was a terrible father, and a worst husband. When you are in the midst of sin it can be difficult to see yourself as others see you. The old prison where I was housed gave me a reality check. Prior to the sentence I wore expensive clothing, drank expensive liquor, and partied with expensive women. In the old English prison I had to wear prison issued clothing, I was locked up with a bunch of men, and the only liquor in the prison was the cheap moonshine the prisoners brewed.

Some of us are so hard headed it takes a midnight crisis to wake us up. I know there are many people who are dealing with dark situations that came upon them because they failed to heed warning signs. I know beyond a shadow of a doubt that prior to being arrested in England; I was on a crash course with death and destruction. God allowed the arrest in England to be a detour where He could speak to my heart and introduce me to His son Jesus Christ. Although I faced a lengthy prison sentence in England and the United States, I realized that God had spared my life and was giving me an opportunity to turn my life around. If you are reading this from a physical prison, take a moment and think about the number of times you were warned to stop doing what you were doing. When I was in those dark places, my mind began to go over all the times I was warned. I knew I had no one to blame but myself. Being locked up in small quarters with a stranger for a cell mate was stressful enough, but being away from my family made the situation more desperate.

I took time to read the Bible in order to pass time but eventually I developed a deep interest in what I read. Once I was exposed to the truth of the word I realized that I was ignorant to the things of God, and had some false ideas about who Jesus was. The word of God made me realize the level of darkness that permeated my life. That is what the word does; it acts as a plum line or measuring rod. It will show us the areas in our lives where we are going astray. Although prison was a dark place and my imprisonment was a dark period, a light began to shine on March, 6 1991.

Four months after my arrest I surrendered my heart to the Lord Jesus while reading the book of John. The pivotal moment came as I read John five, verses 39 and 40. The darkness of my incarceration gave way to the marvelous light of the Lord Jesus. You can be in a dark environment when you are facing or serving a long prison sentence, when you have been diagnosed with a terminal illness, or when you have received news of the sudden death of a loved one. At the darkest point of your crisis you will have to decide whether or not you are going to fight or flee. The literal prison bars were still there when Jesus came into my heart, but spiritually I was free. A song writer declared, *"I am free. Praise the Lord I am free. No longer bound, no more chains holding me, praise the Lord, Hallelujah I'm free."* When the Son sets you free, you are free indeed. You are free from the bondage of sinful deeds because He frees your mind from the power of sin.

Life begins when Jesus enters our lives. Before He enters our lives, we merely exist. When He comes in we find purpose, we find the true meaning of life, and we find the Zoë, the God kind of life, the abundant life, Hallelujah!!! We must have a will to live for Him, *"For God, who commanded the light to shine out of darkness, hath shined in our hearts, to give the light of the knowledge of the glory of God in the face of Jesus Christ. But we have this treasure in earthen vessels, that the excellency of the power may be of God, and not of us" (2 Corinthians 4:6).* Our vessels are fragile but with Jesus Christ dwelling on the inside, our vessels can bring glory to God. He brings His light to our dark souls, and His light illuminates a previously dark and marred vessel. God allows the treasure to be in fragile earthly vessels so the vessel will not take the glory for itself, but it will give all to Him.

When the crisis of the midnight hour comes, allow the Lord to command light to shine out of that dark place. Fight the encroachment of sadness, depression, and melancholy. Fight the encroachment of spirits of suicide and homicide. Allow the Father of lights to get glory out of the situation. When Jesus came to dwell on the throne of my heart on March, 6 1991, my primary concern was not when I would get out of prison. My primary concern was allowing Him to use me in the prison to be a light shining in a dark place. When I was sentenced to eight years I had peace because the Lord had saved me before I received the sentence. When we are in Christ we will not be exempt from midnight seasons, but He will prepare and strengthen us in those seasons. The peace of God can and will guard our hearts and minds during the darkest hour of the crisis. Jailhouse religion cannot keep you in the midnight hour. As a matter of fact religion can only bind you, it cannot give you freedom. A covenant relationship with Jesus is what will transform the darkest atmosphere. You have to be sincere in your desire to walk with Him. You have to renounce all sin, and ask Him to help you to die to the flesh daily.

I was able to face the music of the eight year sentence because I surrendered my will to Jesus and had total confidence that He would do what was best for me. There were challenges throughout the course of the sentence, but I faced each of them with the confidence the Lord gave me. I dedicated myself to the work of the Lord in the prison and He gave me favor with the case in the United States. When men said no parole for my offense, God opened the prison doors in England, three years after I arrived. The eight year sentence represented a new beginning for me because eight is the number of new beginnings. The three years that I served was symbolic of resurrection because the number three is symbolic of resurrection and divine completion. Prison was like a grave but Jesus resurrected me and started me on the path to perfection.

I arrived in England spiritually dead, but I received a new lease on life and became a new creature in Christ. The situation looked dark and bleak at the beginning but I persevered with the help of God until I learned to walk in the light. Jesus Christ is the only one who can keep you strong in the midnight hour until the light of day is visible. He can do it because He came to destroy the works of darkness. We have to be brave enough to cast our cares on Him and allow Him to be God in our lives. It does not stay dark forever. The darker your situation becomes the closer you are to the light. At the darkest point of the crisis you may feel like you are alone, but you must find Christ in the crisis. There are times when friends and family will not be able to go all the way with us but we must take comfort in the fact that

"Jesus will never leave us or forsake us." He has given us promises, and His promises will never fail.

Everywhere I go, I try to share my testimony with others, and how the Lord turned my mourning into dancing. He gave me the garment of praise to substitute the spirit of heaviness. Our testimony can help others who are going through things Jesus has helped us through, or delivered us from. When the Lord opened the prison door for me and tuned my midnight into a breakthrough, in my heart I decided to be an instrument in His hands. I know we do not like people to know about our sordid past. Without a past we would not have a present or a future. He took false pride away from me, so I would have no problem telling people that Jesus delivered me in the midst of an eight year prison sentence. He delivered me from a life of alcohol and drug dealing. Sin is a prison where people are bound. A person might not have experienced a literal prison, but every person has something in their life they wrestle with. Jesus can set you free, if you are willing to cry out to Him.

If you are dealing with a midnight situation at the present time, take solace in the fact that the men and women of the Bible had to overcome their own midnight trials. The darker your situation, the closer you are to the light of your breakthrough. The Book of Genesis tells us that, *"the evening and the morning were the first day."* During the creation of the world, evening comes before morning. This means you have to persevere through the evening to get to the morning. In the history of creation chronicled in the book of Genesis, darkness was on the face of the deep, the Spirit of God moved upon the face of the waters, God spoke and light began to shine. God saw that the light was good, so He divided the light from the darkness. There are times when we are overcome by dark chaotic situations. It is in those times we must realize the Spirit of God is moving over the face of those situations, and God is about to call for the light to shine.

The depth of the darkness you are dealing with at midnight will determine how close you are to your morning. It will also determine the level of your joy when God brings you through. Whatever your midnight, please be assured that the morning is approaching; with it comes joy, and with joy comes a greater level of strength.

MIDNIGHT MADNESS

An incident took place when Solomon was king and the manner in which he judged the situation showed the people that God had blessed him with great wisdom. Solomon received a visitation from the Lord in the form of a vision. In this vision, God promised to lengthen his days if Solomon kept His statues and commandments as his father David did. When Solomon awoke, he went to Jerusalem. Jerusalem means vision or possession of peace. When we trust in God and allow Him to give us rest in the night, we will have peace when we awake.

After offering burnt offerings and peace offerings before the Ark of the Covenant and making a feast for his servants, Solomon was approached by two harlots. Both women lived in the same house and both had given birth. Three days after one of them delivered her child, the other had her baby. Two is the number of witness and separation. One child died in the night because the mother overlaid it. She was in such a deep and restless sleep that she rolled over and stifled her baby. The mother of the living child spoke to the king concerning the woman with the dead child and said, *"She arose at midnight, and took my son from beside me, while thine handmaid slept, and laid it in her bosom, and laid her dead child in my bosom" (1 Kings 3:20).* She told King Solomon there was no stranger in the house, only the two of them. It appeared as if it was an open and shut case.

The death of the baby was caused by the carelessness of its mother. Instead of taking responsibility for her actions, she used the midnight hour as a cloak to steal the other woman's baby. A mother knows her child and the woman whose baby was stolen knew the dead baby was not hers. We have to be very careful where we lay our heads and who is around us at midnight. This story proves people will commit desperate acts under the cover of darkness. The Bible tells us there is a time coming when a man's foes shall be the people in his own household.

While we are sleeping at midnight, there are spirits working to take things from us that are precious. We have to commune with God on our bed with prayer, praise and worship. We have to make sure there are no un-confessed sins in our lives before we go to sleep at night. We have to detach ourselves from the struggles and challenges of the day and meditate on the Lord and His goodness as we prepare to sleep. It is imperative that we offer up the evening sacrifice and ask the Lord to send angels to guard us in the night. The psalmist declared, *"I laid me down and slept; I awaked; for the LORD sustained me" (Psalm 3:5).*

It seems every time you turn on the news you hear of some child killing their parent(s). Mass murderers seem to be getting younger and younger. We have to make sure there are no open doors in our homes for the grim reaper to enter at midnight. Job said, *"In the dark they dig through houses, which they had marked for themselves in the daytime: they know not the light" (Job 24:16).* The woman who stole the baby was adamant when the accusation was leveled against her. Solomon had to use wisdom to discern who the baby really belonged to. *"And the king said, Bring me a sword. And they brought a sword before the king. And the king said, Divide the living child in tow, and give half to the one, and half to the other" (1 Kings 3:20).* The mother who birthed the child asked the king to give him to the other woman. When she was willing to give up the child, the king knew she was the mother.

There are decisions we will have to make when a midnight crisis is before us and we will have to use discernment and wisdom. In the time of crisis we can not allow ourselves to panic, because there may be people whose lives will be impacted by the decisions we make. We have to seek the Lord for wisdom to judge a situation in the right way. Threatening to cut a baby in half seems crazy, but that is what it took to expose the mother who lied. Do not be surprised if you have to use unconventional means to bring deliverance and expose a lying spirit operating at midnight. As darkness covers the earth people will be faced with grave decisions, and they will look to believers who are operating in a spirit of wisdom for help. We must be ready by the grace of God to give them the answers they need.

Solomon received great wisdom from God because he prayed for it instead of praying for wealth. He received a great foundation from his father David. David went through many wilderness and midnight experiences to get to a place where he could leave a strong foundation for his son Solomon.

PURSUE, OVERTAKE, AND RECOVER

King David faced a midnight situation when he was so depressed by the constant attacks from Saul that he felt he had no other option but live in the land of the Philistines. A believer's situation has to be extremely dark to convince him, that it is better to live in enemy territory than with the people of God. There are many people who have gone back to the enemy territory of the world because they received their greatest pain at the hand of people in the church. Some of them were wounded by leaders. The church is the place where we should receive strength and encouragement, but for some it is the place where they received the deepest wound.

The darkness for David reached its zenith when the Amalekites burned Ziklag with fire and kidnapped the wives and children of David and his men. Ziklag was the territory given to David by a Philistine lord. When David was running from Saul he had to live in caves and in different wildernesses. When he was in the cave of Adullam, people from his father's house came and joined him. Unfortunately they could not help him, because they were dealing with their own midnight crises. In describing the condition of the people who joined him the Bible declares, *"And every one that was in distress, and everyone that was in debt, and everyone that was discontented, gathered themselves unto him; and he became a captain over them: and there were with him about four hundred men"* (1 Samuel 22:2).

It is tough enough when you are dealing with your own problems, but things are more difficult when you have to bear the burden of others at the same time. God allowed him to be captain over the people who were in debt, and discontented to teach him to lead from the ground up. As king he would have to be able to identify with people who were suffering. Have you ever found yourself in a place where you were struggling to pay your own debts but had to find money to help others who were in a worse situation than you were? Have you ever found yourself encouraging people who were discontented when you needed encouragement yourself? There are times when we make great sacrifices for others only to be attacked by those same people.

David's lowest point in the midnight crisis came when Ziklag was burned by the Amalekites and the very people whom he helped spoke of stoning him, because their wives and children were taken captive. David and all the men who were with him wept until they had no more power to weep. When they had no more tears to shed the men turned on David. It is very painful when the people who should stand with you in the time of crisis are the ones picking up stones to throw at you. It is very painful when believers in the body of Christ, believers in your own church, are the ones hurling the stones of accusation and criticism at you. Many people have not been able to bounce back from the blows suffered at the hands of people who were supposed to be supportive.

David's response to the crisis can teach us a valuable lesson if we allow it to. The Bible describes David's condition as being, "greatly distressed." He had to dig deep down to survive the catastrophe. *1 Samuel 30:6* ends with these words, *"But David encouraged himself in the LORD his God."* We can not avoid the coming of some midnight situations because God allows trials in our lives to teach us, to strength us, and to get us to trust Him in dark times. The question is not a matter of if but when we will have to deal with a midnight situation. The key to survival is, we have to find a way to encourage ourselves in the Lord our God when the crisis is so dark we do not know which way to turn. David could have allowed himself to be defeated by the situation. He was already battling the despair of being attacked by Saul, and chased out of the land he loved. Always remember that the darkest hour comes before the light begins to breakthrough. It is the enemy's desire to get us to give up at that point. Instead of quitting, David spoke to Abiathar the priest and requested the ephod. The ephod was the instrument the priests wore when they went before the Lord. It is comforting to know that we have a high priest who took our infirmities, and bore our grief.

He consulted with the LORD and asked the LORD two questions. *"Shall I pursue after this troop? Shall I overtake them?"* God gave him three answers because God is a God of overflow and increase. God told him to, *"Pursue: for thou shalt surely overtake them, and without fail recover all."* David found an Egyptian in a field who was left for dead by his Amalekite master. David fed him and when he regained his strength he told David where the enemy was. God is so awesome. He can use anything or anyone to be a blessing to us, even someone the enemy has left for dead. When he led David to the Amalekites they were eating, drinking, and dancing because of the great spoil they had taken out of Ziklag and Judah. The devil and his minions might be partying at the present time, because they have stolen husbands, wives, children, health, and other valuable things from us. But we need to tell the devil that the party is over, because we shall surely overtake him and recover all.

David smote them and recovered everything and everyone. Do not sink into despair and depression because your midnight crisis has reached its apex. Arise from the place of despondency and pursue the enemy. Rise up with a sense of determination and make up your mind that the devil will not keep the children he has stolen, the wife or the husband he has stolen, and he will not keep anything or any person he has stolen. We have to fight him with fasting and prayer. Once we locate his territory we can use radical praise to break up his demonic party. If you are in a place of despair at the present time rise up and praise God so that you can work to ambush the enemy. David declared, *"At midnight I will rise to give thanks unto thee because of thy righteous judgments" (Psalm 119:62).* The righteous judge is on our side and when we pursue in His name we must overtake the enemy, and we must recover all.

IS JESUS THE ONE: YES HE IS!!!

John the Baptist had an awesome ministry. He rejoiced in his mother Elisabeth's womb when he heard the voice of Jesus' mother Mary. He came in the spirit of Elijah to prepare the way for Jesus the Messiah, who happened to be his cousin. He was at the Jordan River baptizing people when Jesus showed up to be baptized in preparation for the start of His ministry. He uttered the famous words, *"Behold the Lamb of God, which taketh away the sin of the world" (John 1:29).* With that one statement he confirmed to the people around that Jesus Christ of Nazareth was sent by God to be the Lamb who would take away the sin of the world. Concerning

John, Jesus said there was none greater born of a woman than he. Despite John's awesome pedigree, family connections, and his anointing as a prophet, he was not excluded from a midnight experience of depression and despair.

His midnight came when he was arrested by Herod and put in prison. John was critical of the relationship between Herod and Herodias. Herod Antipas was an unsavory character. He had eloped with Herodias, the wife of his half brother Philip I. He divorced his own wife and sent her back to her father so he could elope with Herodias. John told him that it was not lawful to have his brother's wife. That is not what Herod or Herodias wanted to hear. When the daughter of Herodias danced before Herod on his birthday, he promised to give her whatsoever she wanted. Her mother had instructed her to ask for the head of John Baptist on a charger. *"Hell hath no fury like a woman's scorn."*

John was arrested and put in prison. He sat in prison with a death sentence hanging over his head. Talk about a midnight situation. He was used to ministering in the wilderness, so it must have been very difficult for him to be shut up in prison. There are great spiritual leaders in the Bible who felt like quitting due to doubt and uncertainty. Moses, Elijah, and Jeremiah all thought about giving up, even the Apostle Paul despaired about his life at one point. Do not feel guilty if you have felt that way at one time or another. If you have an anointing on your life, especially a prophetic anointing, you will have to battle spirits of depression that will come at you in varying degrees. The emotional and physical strain of being imprisoned for months took their toll on John and caused him to doubt. Is the physical and emotional strain you have dealt with over the last few months or years causing you to doubt? Is it a financial, a marital, or a strain of infirmity? Doubting is normal in the time of extreme suffering but do not allow doubt to turn into unbelief. Doubt arises when we cannot understand what the Lord is doing and why He is doing it. Unbelief is a refusal to believe God's Word, to take Him at His promise, and to obey His instructions.

While sitting in prison John's disciples told him about all the wonderful works of Jesus among the people. *"And John calling unto him two of his disciples sent them to Jesus, saying, Art thou he that should come? Or look we for another" (Luke 12:58)?"* John's midnight crisis caused him to doubt who Jesus was. It is imperative that we keep sight of Jesus and know who He is in the midst of the storm. He does not change; *"He is the same yesterday today and forever."* I cannot help but wonder if John doubted because Jesus was doing miracles amongst the people while he languished in prison awaiting execution. John might have wondered why he was not delivered from the prison if Jesus came to set the captives free. While in the midst of your midnight situation you will see others receiving deliverance and breakthroughs. Do not allow the devil to play tricks on your mind by making you think Jesus is not who the Bible says He is.

When John's disciples asked Jesus the question John sent them to ask him, Jesus answered by saying, *"Go your way, and tell John what things ye have seen and heard; how that the blind see, the lame walk, the lepers are cleansed, the deaf hear, the dead are raised, to the poor the gospel is preached. And blessed is he, whosoever shall not be offended in me" (Luke 12:22-23).* Actions speak louder than words, so Jesus did not spend time explaining His credentials to John's disciples. He did not give them a lecture on theology and prophecy; He simply allowed them to be eyewitnesses of the miracles being wrought among the people. The miracles performed among the people confirmed His credentials as the promised Messiah.

Could it be possible that John's midnight crisis caused him to be offended in Jesus? Jesus' last words to John's disciples are very revealing. *"Blessed is he, whosoever shall not be offended in me."* According to the online PC Bible Study, "The Greek word translated "offended" gives us our English word *scandalize*, and it referred originally to the "bait stick" in a trap. John was in danger of being trapped because of his concern about what Jesus was not doing. He was stumbling over his Lord and His ministry." We should never be under the false notion that Jesus is not working because our deliverance has not manifested.

As soon as John's disciples left, Jesus began to speak to the People concerning John. He told them that John was not a reed shaken with the wind. John was not arrayed in soft raiment, and gorgeous apparel; He did not live delicately like a king in his court. He said John was much more than a prophet. He was a messenger sent by God to prepare the way for Jesus. After he told them of John's credentials, Jesus said something very interesting to the people. *"For I say unto you, among those that are born of women there is not a greater prophet than John the Baptist: but he that is least in the kingdom of God is greater than he" (Luke 12:20).* I wonder if the least in the kingdom is greater than John because they kept their faith In Jesus to the end. They were not born with the reputation, the anointing, and the prophetic calling of John, but they were able to keep their eyes focused on Jesus.

We have to be like the three Hebrew boys when we are in the heat of midnight. They refused to bow to the king's idol when he threatened them with the fiery furnace. They knew God could deliver them but they told the king, that even if God did not deliver them, they would not bow. There is a great temptation to bow when the heat is turned up but we must remain steadfast. We have to ask the Holy Ghost to search us daily to determine if we are offended in Jesus. We have to trust the sovereignty of God and know that if we are not healed here on earth, we are guaranteed to be healed by the time we are taken into His presence. God's will has to be done in the earth and that means we will have to endure trials. Faith and trust means we will not look back when we feel He is not moving fast enough. John the Baptist was a great man but even great men have feet that are made of clay. The greater the man the more fragile the clay and for this reason great men must trust in Jesus.

When facing storms or any type of crisis we can learn a great deal from the heroes of faith listed in the book of Hebrews. Moses refused to be called the son of Pharaoh's daughter, but chose to suffer affliction with the people of God rather than enjoy the pleasures of sin for a season. He esteemed the reproach of Jesus Christ's riches, which were greater than the treasures in Egypt, for he had respect unto the recompense of the reward. The harlot Rahab did not perish with the unbelievers of Jericho because she risked her life and received the spies with peace. The men and women who have gone before us were able to subdue kingdoms, and stop the mouths of lions. They were tortured and did not accept deliverance because they desired a better resurrection. They suffered all of these things in faith because they believed God. We have to continue to fight the good fight of faith because we are compassed about with a great cloud of witnesses.

When the battle gets tough and you feel like quitting, send up praise, thank the Lord for allowing you to endure affliction for the sake of the gospel. He will never put more upon us than we are able to bear. Midnight is not an hour for the weak or the faint of heart. Many people quit in the midnight hour because doubt and fear seize them and they feel as if they can not go on.

WATCH YOUR STEP

The Psalmist Asaph wrote, *"Truly God is good to Israel, even to such as are of a clean heart. But as for me, my feet were almost gone; my steps had well nigh slipped. For I was envious at the foolish, when I saw the prosperity of the wicked" (Psalm 73:1-3).* It can be very discouraging when you see people prosper who are not interested in serving the Lord. Asaph had to endure a midnight crisis while he watched the ungodly prosper. Asaph said, *"For all the day long have I been plagued, and chastened every morning. When I thought to know this it was too painful for me" (Psalm 73: 14, 16).* I love what he wrote in the 17th verse. "Until I went into the sanctuary of God; then understood I their end." The Hebrew word used in Psalm 73 for sanctuary is *miqdash;* it means *a consecrated thing or place, especially a palace; a chapel, a hallowed place.* Find that consecrated place in the midnight hour and allow Jehovah-mekoddishkem to give you peace.

On page 92 of her book: *The Peace & Power of Knowing God's Name,* Author Kay Arthur wrote, *"The death of Christ provides for our redemption, for 'without shedding of blood thee is no forgiveness' of sins (Hebrews 9:22). The resurrection of Christ provides us with the ability to walk in newness of life through the gift of the Holy Spirit who sets us free from the law of sin and death (Romans 6:4; 8:2-4). The God who sanctified Israel is the God who sanctifies the church. The God who carried His people "on eagles' wings" is the God who carries you and me. Call on His name and enter into His wonderful rest."*

When Jesus taught His disciples to pray, He told them to hallow His Father's name. The Greek word for hallow is *hagiazo;* it means to *make holy, to purify or consecrate.* Proverbs 18:10 declares, *"The name of the LORD is a strong tower: the righteous runneth into it, and is safe."* He is Elohim: The Creator, El Elyon: The God Most High, El Roi: The God Who sees, El Shaddai: The All-Sufficient One, Adonai: The Lord, Jehovah: The Self-Existent One, Jehovah-jireh: The LORD That Provides, Jehovah-rapha: The LORD Our Healer, Jehovah-nissi: The LORD Our Banner, Jehovah-mekoddishkem: The LORD Who Sanctifies Us, Jehovah-shalom: The LORD Is Peace, Jehovah-sabaoth: The LORD Of Hosts, Jehovah-raah: The LORD Our Shepherd, Jehovah-tsidkenu: The LORD Our Righteousness, Jehovah-shammah: The LORD Is There.

The Father has rolled all these characteristics and attributes and put them into one name and that is the name of Jesus Christ. Paul told the Philippians that *"God also hath highly exalted him, and given him a name which is above every name: That at the name of Jesus every knee should bow, of things in heaven, and things in earth, and things under the earth; And that every tongue should confess that Jesus Christ is Lord, to the glory of God the Father."* Paul uses the Greek word *kurios* for Lord. It means supreme in authority, God and master. Many religions want us to believe Jesus was just a good man or a prophet, but He is all that and more. He is either Lord of all or He is not Lord at all. In the darkness of our midnight hour, we can rest in the knowledge that Jesus is the supreme authority, God, and He is the Master.

When Jesus and His disciples came into coasts of Caesarea Philippi He asked His disciples a very important question, *"Whom do men say that I the Son of man am"* *(Matthew 16:13)?* There were many different religions in the area. It was the center of Baal worship in the past. There were shrines erected to the Greek god pan, and Herod the great built his temple there in honor of Augustus Caesar. It was in the midst of that pagan territory that Peter received the revelation of who Jesus was. Once you have the revelation of who Jesus is, you will be able to put your midnight situation in its proper perspective. When Jesus asked the question the disciples told Him some of the people thought He was John the Baptist, while others thought He was Elias, others thought He was Jeremiah, or one of the prophets.

People are just as confused today about His identity as people were when He walked the earth. When Jesus made the question personal by asking His disciples who they thought He was, Simon Peter answered and said, *"Thou art the Christ, the Son of the living*

God" *(Matthew 13:16).* If we are going to walk in victory we have to know beyond a shadow of a doubt that God has made Jesus both Lord and Christ. We must have the revelation that Peter received. We can not receive the revelation of Jesus from flesh and blood. Only the Father in heaven can reveal the real Jesus Christ to us.

Jesus told Peter that he would receive keys to the kingdom of heaven. He was giving Peter the authority to bind and loosen things in heaven and earth. Once the revelation of Jesus is received from the Father, we will have the authority to bind and loosen. Jesus told Peter that He was building His church and the gates of hell would not prevail against it. The church of Jesus Christ is not a building made with the hands of men. It is the *ekklesia.* This word was used to describe an assembly of Greek citizens who helped to govern a city or district. The church of Jesus Christ is a called out people who are being perfected to rule, reign and carry His glory. We are being perfected in the furnace of affliction. The midnight situations we have to face are building strength and godly character in us. Do not fight the night, just praise Jesus Christ, give Him all the glory.

In the Bible gates represent authority and power. Important business was transacted at the city gate. When Jesus said the "Gates of hell would not prevail against His Church" He was saying that Satan and his most powerful demons will not prevail against us because we are His building; we are His temple, and the work of His hands. He is the wise Master Builder, and He is building us on a firm foundation that can not be destroyed. The devil will use other religions to come against the name of Jesus but believers must never compromise when it comes to the authority of the name of Jesus. He is God manifested in the flesh.

The next time some Jehovah's witnesses come to your door, do not hide and pretend you are not home. Open your door and take them to *Philippians 2: 5-11.* Show them why they need to have the mind of Christ. When they tell you that you should be using the name Jehovah, tell them that Jehovah has highly exalted Him and given Him a name that is above every name. If they truly love Jehovah then they will use the name of Jesus, because that is the name Jehovah has highly exalted. That is the name that is above every name.

Cancer is a name but it is not greater than the name of Jesus Christ. Diabetes is a name but it is not greater than the name of Jesus Christ. Alzheimer is a name but it is not greater than the name of Jesus Christ. Schizophrenia is a name but it is not greater than the name of Jesus Christ. Dementia is a name but it is not greater than the name of Jesus Christ. Lupus is a name but it is not greater than the name of Jesus. Fibromyalgia is a name but it is not greater than the name of Jesus. Acquired Immune Deficiency Syndrome (AIDS) is a name but it is not greater than the name of Jesus Christ. Midnight is a name but it is not greater than the name of Jesus Christ. Whatever the sickness, whatever the disease, and whatever the infirmity you are facing today, call on the name of Jesus Christ because His name is exalted above every name. HALLELUJAH. LET THE NAME OF THE LORD BE PRAISED!!!

His name is the name you can call in the midnight hour; the name that will calm your fears and dry your tears. It is the name that makes demons tremble. Call on the name of Jesus Christ. Call on the name of Yeshua the Mesheach. He will bless you and keep you in the midnight hour. He will make His face to shine upon you and be gracious unto you; He will lift up his countenance upon you and grant you peace. He is the Prince of Peace, Yeshua Ha-Mesheach Sar Shalom.

THE KINSMAN REDEEMER

At midnight Boaz was afraid when he felt something moving by his feet. When he looked to see what it was, he saw a woman by his feet. When he inquired about her situation, he realized it was a damsel and her name was Ruth. She asked him to spread his skirt over her because he was a near kinsman. Boaz is a type of the Lord Jesus Christ in that he is the kinsman redeemer. Ruth is a type of bride because she is in the place of intimacy with the kinsman redeemer. Boaz had come from harvesting at the threshing floor and retired after eating and drinking. Ruth came and uncovered his feet and lay down. To uncover the feet was an act of intimacy. Being at the feet speaks of humility along with intimacy. Mary the sister of Lazarus sat at the feet of Jesus. Mary Magdalene brought an alabaster box into a house where Jesus was and washed His feet with her tears, wiped them with the hairs of her head, and kissed His feet and anointed them with precious ointment.

During this time period, an individual would spread their mantle over another to claim them as their own. Elijah passed by Elisha and cast his mantle upon him. Elisha then left his oxen and ran after Elijah (1 Kings 19:19). The word skirt also translates to mean wing. *"He shall cover thee with his feathers, and under his wings shalt thou trust: his truth shall be thy shield and buckler" (Psalm 91:4).* He told Ruth to tarry that night and he would perform his part as a kinsman, in the morning. He told her to lie down until morning, so she lay at his feet until morning. God will give us rest in the night. He does not want us to be tormented at midnight. We can rest in the night in preparation for the redemption He will provide in the morning. She rested at his feet and rose early in the morning, and he blessed her with provision of barley. He refused to send her back to her mother in-law empty handed.

Although he was troubled at the stirring by his feet at midnight, Boaz accepted Ruth. Boaz promised to do what she requested, because all the people knew she was a virtuous woman. There is an interesting thing to note here. There was a kinsman who was nearer than Boaz and he had a prior claim on her. When it was time to speak to the man, Boaz went up to the gate where business transactions were conducted. He called together ten of Bethlehem's elders to serve as witnesses to the legal transaction. Bethlehem means house of bread. The number ten is symbolic of law, order, and restoration. Ruth was a widow who lived with her mother in-law Naomi, who was also a widow. Widows needed to be sustained. By marrying Ruth it meant both her and Naomi would receive bread which is a form of sustenance from Boaz. The marriage represented a time of restoration and order. But first, the nearer kinsman would have to agree.

Boaz instructed the man that Naomi had a field for sale that belonged to her late husband. The death of her husband and her two sons put her in poverty so she needed to sell the land. The nearer kinsman had the first right to the property, and Boaz was next after him. The man agreed to redeem the land. But Boaz explained to him that by redeeming the land, he must also acquire Ruth the Moabitess. He would have to marry her in order to raise a son to carry the family name. When the man heard about marriage, he refused his right of purchase. Many men are willing to go along for the ride until they hear about marriage, then they get cold feet and back away. Ladies, do not give away the milk for free, because a lot of men will not buy the cow if they do not have to pay for milk. Wait for your Boaz because you can mess up your destiny by marrying the wrong man. Ruth was a Moabite, but she had virtue. The Moabites were the people who came from Lot's incestuous relationship with his daughter when he was in a drunken stupor. But, God is a redeemer and He will not hold our background against us.

Jesus is coming back for a bride without spot, wrinkle, or blemish-- a bride of virtue. His death, burial, and resurrection took care of everything required to save us and prepare us for the marriage. As His brides, we have to remain in a place of sanctification and consecration. It is in that place that we will be covered and protected at midnight.

Boaz was able to redeem Ruth for the Bible declares, *"So Boaz took Ruth, and she was his wife: and when he went in unto her, the LORD gave her conception, and she bore a son" (Ruth 4:13).*

The encounter between Boaz and Ruth started out at midnight with Boaz being afraid, but it went from fear to blessings. We never hear the name of the near kinsman redeemer, and after the transaction he disappears from the scriptures. But, out of the marriage between Boaz and Ruth came Obed the father of Jesse who was the father of King David. The lineage runs all the way to Joseph, Mary and Jesus. Our Lord and Savior Jesus Christ is the true kinsman redeemer. We do not need to look to another because he has purchased us with His blood. When we were in the world and in sin, the devil was the nearer kinsman but he had us bound. We were like the Moabites in that we were born in sin, but our Kinsman redeemer, the last Adam has wiped the slate clean with His precious blood and now our name is written in the Lambs book of life like the name of Ruth is written in the genealogy of Jesus.

Our midnight may start as a time of fear and trembling as it did for Boaz but we never know what God can bring out of it. But, if we trust Him he will get the glory out of it.

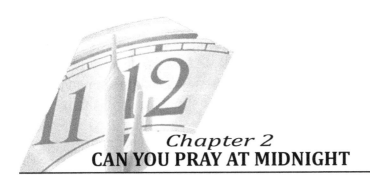

Chapter 2
CAN YOU PRAY AT MIDNIGHT

There are principles and keys in the scriptures that will help the believer to overcome the obstacles they encounter on their journey to perfection in Jesus Christ. We have to search the scriptures in-order to obtain these principles and keys. *"It is the glory of God to conceal a thing: but the honor of kings is to search out a matter" (Proverbs 25:2).* Jesus spoke these words to the Apostle Peter, *"And I will give unto thee the keys of the kingdom of heaven: and whatsoever thou shalt bind on earth shall be bound in heaven: and whatsoever thou shalt loose on earth shall be loosed in heaven" (Matthew 16:19).* Jesus had the authority to give Peter the keys because Revelation 1:18 declares, *"I am he that liveth, and was dead; and, behold, I am alive for evermore, Amen; and have the keys of hell and of death."* Random House Webster's Collegiate Dictionary defines the word key as, *"something that controls entrance to a place, a small metal instrument specially cut to fit into a lock and move its bolt;" something that affords a means to achieve, master, or understand something."*

The key to success for our Christian journey is the ability to understand and obey the principles found in the scriptures through the power of the Holy Ghost. A lack of understanding of the word of God will cause us to grope in the darkness, and to be susceptible to false doctrine. The Apostle Paul told his spiritual son Timothy to, *"Study to show thyself approved unto God, a workman that needeth not to be ashamed, rightly dividing the word of truth" (2 Timothy 2:15).*

One of the keys to breakthrough and deliverance when dealing with a midnight situation is prayer. We should not wait for a midnight crisis to come upon on us before we pray. We should have an active, vibrant prayer life that we can tap into once midnight arrives. In most instances the midnight crisis will come upon us suddenly and without warning. That is not the time to stumble around wondering what we should pray. We should already have a seasoned prayer life and a level of maturity that allows us to withstand the initial blow without falling apart completely.

The midnight prayer has to be intense, because the opposition coming against us at midnight will be intense. "Now I lay me down to sleep" is not a bad prayer, but we will have to go deeper in the midnight hour. Midnight is a time where warfare prayers will be necessary. It will be a time of binding and loosing. It is a time where we will have to turn down our plates and fast because the type of opposition we face will be akin to the ones Jesus declared "will only come out by prayer and fasting." When you search the scriptures you will encounter many instances when God's people were faced with midnight situations and were able to overcome through prayer. We can learn from these individuals if we apply the principles of prayer as they did when faced with opposition.

HANNAH PRAYED

Hannah was one of the wives of a man named Elkanah. Her name means woman of favor or grace, and she would need both favor and grace from the Lord to deal with her midnight situation which was barrenness. Grace is not only God's unmerited favor, it is His divine enablement. God told the Apostle Paul that His grace was sufficient for him because His strength was made perfect in weakness. You can have the favor and grace of the Lord on your life and still have to deal with barrenness for certain seasons. Elkanah gave Hannah a worthy portion of meat because he loved her; although she was loved by her husband the Bible says, *"But the LORD had shut up her womb" (1 Samuel 1:5).* God allows this in-order to strengthen our prayer life, and to build trust, character and integrity in us. He also does it so we will not birth out of due season. He has us on a timetable for His purpose and there are certain things that will not be birthed until He is ready for His plan to be fulfilled. We have to be able to discern

28

when a barren situation is from the Lord and trust Him to turn the barrenness into fruitfulness in His season.

Hannah had not been able to conceive children. In Old Testament times a childless woman was considered a failure. Her barrenness was a stigma and a social embarrassment for her husband. Children were an integral part of the society's economic structure. They were a source of labor for the family and were required to take care of their parents in their old age. If a wife was not able to bear children, ancient Middle Eastern Custom allowed her to give one of her servant girls to her husband to bear children for her. We see an example of this in the case of Abram, his wife Sarai, and her maid Hagar. All things are lawful but not all things are expedient. Just because something is an acceptable custom does not mean God is pleased with it.

Elkanah could have left Hannah because of her barrenness. A husband was allowed to divorce a barren wife. Despite social criticism and the civil law, Elkanah remained devoted to Hannah. Elkanah had a second wife named Peninnah and she was able to bear him many children.

Every year Elkanah took his family to Shiloh to worship and they sat down to eat a meal as part of that worship. Instead of enjoying the time of worship Hannah was sad because Peninnah used it as an opportunity to torment her about her barrenness. Hagar despised Sarah when she bore Ishmael. Peninnah was ruthless in her attacks and torment of Hannah.

"And her adversary also provoked her sore, for to make her fret, because the LORD had shut up her womb. And as he did so year by year, when she went up to the house of the LORD, so she provoked her; therefore she wept, and did not eat" (1 Samuel 1:6-7). They lived in the same house but they were adversaries, they worshipped in the same church but they were adversaries. Some of our toughest critics and tormentors are in the same house and the same church with us. They attack us and criticize us because there are areas in our lives that have not produced fruit.

The adversary is brazen enough to try and depress and oppress God's people right in the sanctuary. It is a travesty when the people of God are unable to enjoy worship because there is barrenness in their lives and they are being tormented by other people in the body. It is amazing how cruel and small minded people can be. People of the household of faith should support and edify each other, not criticize and tear down each other. Elkanah gave Hannah a generous portion but it could not compensate for her barrenness. Life can seem unfair at times.

Peninnah had a nasty attitude yet she was able to have children while Hannah the woman of God was barren. There are things in the kingdom of God that are mysteries. It is difficult to comprehend why the wicked appear to prosper while godly men struggle, why some evil men seem to live long lives, while some godly men die early. We have to trust the plan of God because He sees things perfectly clear while wee see through a dimly lit glass. God uses barrenness in scripture for His Glory. Sarai was barren but God caused her to laugh when He opened her womb and gave her Isaac the child of promise. Once she birthed the promised child He changed her name from Sarai to Sarah which signified she would be the mother of nations. The Lord will keep you barren for a season as He prepares you to birth something or someone who will change nations. Isaac entreated the LORD for his wife Rebekah because she was barren. The word entreated in Hebrew is *athar (pronounced aw-thar)* and it means to burn incense in worship, to intercede. The LORD heard Isaac's worship and intercessory prayer and his wife conceived. When you are barren you do not need people in your life who are going to speak out of their flesh; you need people who will worship, lift up supplication and intercession unto the Lord for you. Many marriages have ended because one spouse was barren. Instead of divorce court the fertile spouse should have intreated the Lord for the barren one.

Prayer, praise and worship will cause barren wombs and testis to become fertile. Isaac's son Jacob had a wife named Rachel and she was barren. *"And God remembered Rachel, and God hearkened to her, and opened her womb. And she conceived, and bare a son; and said, God hath taken away my reproach: and she called his name Joseph; and said, The Lord shall add to me another son" (Genesis 30:22). Joseph would go on to be a great leader in Egypt who God used to feed nations.* Manoah's wife was barren but after an Angelic visitation she conceived and bore Samson. Zacharias and his wife Elisabeth were both righteous before God, they walked in all His commandments, ordinances and were blameless, but they had no child because Elisabeth was barren. The Bible says, *"while he executed the priest's office before God in the order of his course, according to the custom of the priest's office, his lot was to burn incense when he went into the temple of the Lord. And the whole multitude of the people were praying without at the time of incense. And there appeared unto him an angel of the Lord standing on the right side of the altar of incense"* (Luke 1:8).

Incense is symbolic of the prayers of the saints. He was standing on the right side of the altar and right is symbolic of blessing and strength. Although his wife was barren and they both were well stricken in age, he continued to serve and to pray. The angel told him his prayer was heard and his wife would bear a son. Do not despise your barrenness; do not allow it to cause you to be derelict in your duty to the Lord because God can and will bring fruitfulness out of it, in His season. *"He maketh the barren woman to keep house, and to be a joyful mother of children. Praise ye the LORD"* (Psalm 113:9). Each individual birthed from a barren womb, would go on to do great things for the Lord. Samson was the only one who I feel, had unfulfilled potential. He did great things by conquering many Philistines, but the lust of his flesh caused him to die an untimely death.

Hannah probably knew the history of Sarah, Rachel, Rebekah, and Samson's mother, how the Lord remembered them and opened their womb. She knew if God did it for her ancestors He could do it for her. Hannah refused to get in the flesh during her midnight crisis of barrenness by responding to Peninnah's taunts. Hannah expressed her anguish to the Lord. When you are in the midnight hour and there is barrenness all around. Do not allow yourself to be drawn into the flesh by the mockers around you; cry out to the Lord for He cares for you and will deliver you.

During one of the meals at Shiloh, Hannah left her family and went into the tabernacle to pray. As mentioned previously, Prayer is a key component to deliverance in your midnight season. Hannah felt in her heart that the Lord wanted her to pray for a son so she could dedicate him to the service of the Lord. As we will see with the prayer of importunity later, we will have to learn to press in prayer. God will not hand us the things we need because we are His children. He is teaching us how to be persistent, consistent, and insistent. The eventual birth of her son would be a key moment in the history of the nation of Israel, but it was facilitated by the fact that, Hannah prayed.

Can you rise from depression, despair, and the melancholy of your midnight situation to pray effectually and fervently? It is very easy to fall into a state of despair and depression because you are facing a barren situation, but please remember, if you can persevere and press in prayer, God can birth something out of you that will change the course and the destiny of nations. There are many people that can trace their deliverance to a praying mother, grandmother, sister or father. Although she was experiencing bitterness of soul, Hannah arose from the place of despair, entered the tabernacle and prayed. She was so burdened in her soul that her lips moved but no sound came out as she prayed. Prayer is not about how many words we can speak out of our mouth, it is not about how we look or sound to those around us. Prayer is about reaching deep down into our hearts to pour out to God.

John Bunyan declared, *"In prayer it is better to have a heart without words, than words without a heart."* The priest Eli thought Hannah was drunk and told her to *"put away thy wine from thee."* It is a shame when the priest can not discern the difference between a drunk and someone who is pouring out their soul before the Lord. Do not expect the religious people around you to understand your zeal to connect to the Lord in prayer. Do not be deterred by their misguided criticism when they are unable to discern your midnight cry unto your God Yahweh. Press pass their criticisms and baseless mocking because your Father in heaven knows your heart and He can hear the cry of your heart. No one can understand the depth of the pain that comes from a barren womb that desires to be fruitful, only the individual who have suffered the indignity of the barrenness truly knows the sorrow associated with it.

You may feel the desperate pain of bareness because your biological clock is ticking, and you have lived with loneliness for many years, due to your inability to find a suitable spouse. You may have found the spouse but your bareness is a loveless marriage which saw the departure of luster many years ago. Whatever the cause of your barrenness; please hold on because your season of fruitfulness is on the way. Hannah spoke these words to Eli, *"No, my lord, I am a woman of a sorrowful spirit: I have drunk neither wine nor strong drink, but have poured out of my soul before the LORD. Count not thine handmaid for a daughter of Belial: for out of the abundance of my complaint and grief have I spoken hitherto" (1 Samuel 1:15).* When Eli realized she was not drunk but that she prayed to the Lord, he blessed her and told her that God would grant her petition. There are times people will not understand your posture in prayer, but you do not change because of a lack of understanding on the part of others, even if the person is a leader. Once they get an understanding they will speak a blessing over you.

On the day of Pentecost the disciples were mocked by some of the devout men who were gathered at Jerusalem. They accused them of being full of new wine as they left the upper room full of Holy Ghost power and speaking in tongues. They had tarried in prayer and the ensuing result was the baptism of the Holy Ghost. The mockers did not understand that they were full of the wine of the Holy Ghost. When Peter and the eleven stood up with boldness and preached Jesus, they were pricked to the heart and ask, *"What must we do to be saved."* People often criticize the things they do not understand, even moves of God. If it does not fit into their religious mind sets, they are quick to ridicule and criticize. We have to walk in the Spirit and allow God to convict them. We need not get into useless arguments that do not edify God.

When you are seeking the Lord for something you have longed for, you will have to endure the mocking of others and you will have to endure it from people who are believers. Be steadfast and unmovable because God will demonstrate His Glory and they will see the answer to your prayers. When you see the answer to your prayers manifest you will know why the Lord had you to endure and pray in the midnight hour. Hannah's desire for a son was not motivated by her stigma or the torment of Peninnah. She wanted a son so she could dedicate him to the Lord as a Nazarite.

After Eli pronounced the blessing over her she left the tabernacle, got something to eat and her countenance went from sadness to gladness. *"The blessing of the LORD, it maketh rich, and he addeth no sorrow with it" (Proverbs 10:22).* The Hebrew word for blessing in Proverbs 10:22 is berakah. It comes from the word barak; it means benediction, present, prosperity, to kneel. Barrenness causes sorrow, but when the blessing of the Lord comes, there is no sorrow added only joy, and that is why it is worth the wait.

She stepped out on the word from Eli although the manifestation had not come. In the midnight season, just fast, pray, then rejoice and believe God for your answer. It makes no sense to worry if you are going to pray and it makes no sense to pray if you are going to worry. Hannah and her husband rose up early in the morning and worshipped before the Lord before returning to their home at Ramah. The Bible says, *"And Elkanah knew Hannah his wife; and the LORD remembered her. Wherefore it came to pass, when the time was come about after Hannah had conceived, that she bare a son, and called his name Samuel, Because I have asked him of the LORD"* (1 Samuel 1:19b). She withstood the torments of Peninnah, the stigma attached to her infertility, and the rebuke of Eli. She prayed, then worshipped before the Lord in faith and the LORD opened her womb. This is the key principle to deal with your midnight situation. Walk in the fruit of the Spirit, especially when you are being tormented, and criticized. Once you have fasted, prayed, get something to eat then worship before the Lord, as a sign, that you believe by faith, that He has heard your cry and will answer your prayers. The Hebrew word *sa-al* means "asked," and *sama* means "heard;" El is one of the names for God so Samuel means "heard of God" or "asked of God." Whatever you are going through right now, compose yourself, pour out your soul before Him, for He hears and cares for you.

When it was time for the annual trip to Shiloh Hannah received permission from her husband to stay behind and wean Samuel in preparation for his dedication to the service of the Lord. Mothers usually weaned children at the age of three. She told her husband that after the weaning Samuel would *"appear before the LORD, and there abide forever."* The number three is akin to the number seven in that it is symbolic of perfection Divine completion. We were birthed into the body of Jesus Christ and now we are being weaned for third day perfection when we will appear before the Lord to abide in His presence forever. Endure your midnights because there is a great purpose and a plan for your life. You and I are being groomed for a divine appointment.

Elkanah had to agree to Hannah's vow because Jewish law permitted a husband to annul his wife's vow if he disagreed with it (Numbers 30). It must have been very difficult for Elkanah to give up his first born son. According to Exodus 13:11-13, a firstborn son had to be redeemed by a sacrifice but Elkanah gave his first born son Samuel to the Lord as a living sacrifice. The Apostle Paul beseeches the believer to present their bodies to the Lord a living sacrifice.

Parents have hopes and aspirations that their child or children will achieve great success in life. Many parents have a difficult time when it is time for their children to leave the nest. The scriptures instruct parents, "to train up a child in the way that he should go." The way is the narrow way, the way that leads to the kingdom of God. Once they are trained in that way they will not depart. Hannah was barren and if anyone should have held on to their child it should have been her, but she gave him over to the service of the LORD. When God gives you the breakthrough by answering your prayers, please remember to dedicate the thing you receive to Him. Make sure He gets all the glory, all the credit for the good He has done in your life.

Hannah took Samuel along with three bullocks, one ephah of flour, and a bottle of wine. Samuel was young and his life is a testimony to the fact, young people should be dedicated to the work and service of the Lord.

Hannah visited Samuel every year when her family went to Shiloh to worship the LORD with their sacrifices. Samuel became a man of prayer because his mother was a woman who knew how to pray in the midst of a midnight situation. Abraham was willing to offer up Isaac as a sacrifice on mount Moriah. The Apostle Paul told the church at Rome to present their bodies unto the Lord as a living sacrifice.

When they arrived at Shiloh Hannah humbly reminded the priest Eli that she was the woman who stood in the tabernacle and prayed for a son. She had a totally different look on her face and it appears Eli did not recognize her. When it is time for the people who mocked us in our midnight to see the answer to our prayers, we must not be cocky or arrogant. She told Eli that the LORD answered her prayer and as long as Samuel lived he would be lent to the LORD. Lent in Hebrew is different from the way it is used in English. In Hebrew the word is shael (pronounced shaw-al); it means to request, to demand, to obtain leave, and to pray. It is the same Hebrew word used in *Exodus 3:22 and in 11:2* it is used for the word borrow. When the Lord told the Israelites that every man and woman should borrow of his neighbor, jewels of silver, and jewels of gold, they were not expected to pay back the Egyptians. Once Hannah ends her conversation with Eli she offers up a prayer of thanks unto the LORD. *(1 Samuel 2:10)*

"And the child Samuel grew before the LORD" (1 Samuel 20-21). Samuel was a ray of light for the nation of Israel during a dark period. Eli was old and his two sons Hophni and Phinehas were greedy and corrupt. Young Samuel ministered unto the LORD before Eli. *"And the word of the LORD was precious in those days; there was no open vision" (1 Samuel 3:1).* The word for vision here is the same Hebrew word used in *Proverbs 29:18, it is chazown, and it means to see mentally, dream, revelation, and oracle.* Where there is no vision the people will perish. Without light it is impossible to see at night, especially midnight. God gives us vision; He gives us revelation, dreams and oracles so we are able to see mentally when the hour is darkest. Our spiritual lives have to be right so there will be no blockages or hindrances.

The spiritual climate at Shiloh was very dark at that point. The sons of Eli are called sons of Belial because they did not know the LORD. Can you imagine the sons of the priests not knowing the LORD? Their corrupt behavior caused the young men of Israel to sin by abhorring the offering of the LORD. When the head is sick the effect is felt by the entire body. Eli did not discipline his corrupt sons, the people turned away from God so there was no oracle, revelation or dream from the LORD. The state of Eli's eyes gives us a picture of the lack of vision. "His eyes began to wax dim." Contrast Eli's eyes to Moses' eyes when he was old, *"And Moses was an hundred and twenty years old when he died: his eye was not dim, nor his natural force abated" (Deuteronomy 34:7).*

The Bible declares, *"And ere the lamp of God went out in the temple of the LORD, where the ark of God was, and Samuel was laid down to sleep."* The "lamp of God" was the seven-branched golden candlestick that stood in the holy place before the veil, to the left of the golden altar of incense (Exodus 25:31-40; 27:20-21; 37:17-24). The lamp was the only source of light in the holy place. The priests were ordered to keep it burning always. Remember, it is at the entrance of God's word that we receive light so the fact that God was not speaking to his people meant they were living in dark times. The Ark was there, containing the law of God, but it was not beneficial to the people because they did not honor the law. We are modern day priests of the Almighty God and we have to keep our lamps trimmed and full of oil to ensure the light never goes out. It was a sad day in the nation's history when there was no light in the temple. The duty of the priests of God is to ensure the light keeps shining. Whatever you are going through at the moment, do not allow it to dim or to put out your lamp. Let the light shine so others can see the wondrous works of Almighty God and glorify Him.

Eli's poor sight mirrored the lack of a proceeding word from the Lord. It was also indicative of poor leadership. Both Eli and his sons had tragic endings. During one of the battles with the Philistines, the Israelites were defeated so they sent for the Ark of the Covenant out of Shiloh. They felt it could help them win the next battle because the presence of the LORD was there. The problem was, Eli's two sons, Hophni and Phinehas were with the Ark. We can not have corrupt priests who are not sanctified and consecrated handling the presence of the Lord. The people began to shout when the Ark came into the camp. The Bible instructs us to, *"Shout unto God with the voice of triumph,"* but we have to have a consecrated lifestyle behind the shout. The Philistines heard the noise of the shout and realized that the Ark of the LORD was come into the camp. Their response to the coming up of the Ark of the LORD into the camp is very interesting, *"And the Philistines were afraid, for they said, God is come into the camp. And they said, Woe unto us! For there hath not been such a thing heretofore."* *(1 Samuel 4:21).*

Out of their desperation Hophni and Phinehas were trying something new but it would not work because they had contaminated the priests' office. The Philistines understood the power of the God of Israel, because out of their own mouths they declared, *"These are the Gods that smote the Egyptians with all the plagues in the wilderness."* The Philistines slaughtered the Israelites, took the Ark, and killed Hophni and Phinehas. It was truly the midnight hour for the nation, but God never leaves Himself without a witness. When Eli heard the news he was sitting upon a seat by the wayside watching. This should not be the activity of a priest of God when the demonic hordes are attacking God's people. He should not have sat by the wayside watching, he should have been in the temple praying. The Bible declares that, *"his heart trembled for the ark of God."* The Hebrew word for trembled is *hayah*, and it means to break, to faint, to quit. Eli was suffering heart failure, his life was slowly dissipating. Without the presence of the Lord, life is not worth living. He was ninety eight years old at the time and his eyes were so dim he could not see. *Job 17:7 declares, "Mine eye also is dim by reason of sorrow, and all my members are as a shadow."*

Eli was given the news of what had befallen the army of Israel. He was told there was a great slaughter among the people, Hophni and Phinehas were dead, and the ark of God was taken. It must have been a tragic scene. Eli's weak, trembling heart could not bear the brunt of such devastating news. *"And it came to pass, when he made mention of the ark of God, that he fell from the seat backward by the side of the gate, and his neck brake, and he died for he was an old man, and heavy. And he had judged Israel forty years."* It is interesting to note that it was not until he heard the news of the Ark that he fell backward, broke his neck and died. It did not happen when he heard that his sons were dead. The death of his sons was a personal loss but the taking of the Ark of the LORD by the Philistines was a blow to the nation. He fell backward which was not a good direction, he fell by the side of the gate which was not good either. He was old and heavy; he had not kept himself in good shape.

The tragedy for Eli's family did not end with his death and the death of his sons. Phinehas had a wife who was pregnant and about to be delivered of child when she received the news that the Ark of God was taken, and her father in-law and her husband were dead. The birthing should have been a time of joy for her because the women who stood by her told her she was having a son. She was in travail because of the pains that came upon her. When the mid-wives told her not to fear because she had birthed a son, she did not answer or regard them. She named her son Ichabod, "saying, *"the glory is departed from Israel: because the ark of God was taken."* There can be no joy amongst the people when the glory of God has departed. What a dark day that was for the people of God. The Philistines took the Ark from Eben-ezer and brought it to Ashdod into the house of their god

Dagon. Eben-ezer means stone of help. Twenty years later on that very spot, Samuel would set up a memorial stone to commemorate the divine assistance given by God to the Israelites when they routed the Philistines in battle. God needed a faithful priest. A priest He could use to bring deliverance to His people. He used Hannah's barren womb to conceive and birth that priest. Do not despair over your barreness because God has a plan to use it for His Glory.

Samuel was the lone bright spot in the spiritually darkened temple. Although the temple was a dark place during the period of Eli and his sons, Hophni and Phinehas, young Samuel was a little light growing in the midst of gross darkness. The Bible declares, *"But Samuel ministered before the LORD, being a child, girded with a linen ephod."* He was a child but he was dedicated to the LORD before his birth so he knew the importance of focusing on the light of the LORD and not on the apostate priests who surrounded him.

WAIT ON THE LORD AND BE OF GOOD COURAGE

Hannah waited a long time for a man child but the wait was worth it. Waiting is extremely difficult in and of itself. The difficulty is exacerbated when a person is terminally ill or has a loved one who is terminally ill. David tells us to be of good courage while waiting on the Lord because he understood the difficulty inherent in the waiting process. Your posture during the wait will determine your position when you come out of it. Many people experience emotional and physical meltdown while awaiting something important because of the stress on the mind. When we wait on God's timing and He delivers, we can look back and see why waiting was so important.

Hannah waited and her son Samuel became a mighty man of God. Can you imagine how challenging it was for young Samuel to be away from his parents? He had to live with an old man who had fallen out of favor with the LORD. God had Samuel positioned strategically when the people of Israel needed a righteous priest. At a dark period when the lamp of the LORD had gone out at Shiloh, Samuel was the one the LORD called. He was not familiar with the voice of the LORD. He thought Eli called him. We thank God for leaders who can bring us a word from the Lord but we must mature to a place where we can discern His voice for ourselves. It took four calls from God before Eli realized that the LORD was calling young Samuel.

He told Samuel of the judgment that was to come upon the house of Eli. When God turns your bareness into fruitfulness you will look back and discern that all the heartache and the anguish were for a reason and a season. Peninnah had a head start on Hannah in terms of child bearing but Hannah was able to birth a mighty priest, prophet, and Judge for God. Here is what the Word of the Lord declares concerning Samuel, *"And Samuel grew, and the LORD was with him, and did let none of his words fall to the ground. And all Israel from Dan even to Beer-sheba knew that Samuel was established to be a prophet of the LORD. And the LORD appeared again in Shiloh: for the LORD revealed himself to Samuel in Shiloh by the word of the LORD."*

After the birth of Samuel we hear nothing more about Peninnah and her children. Your midnight may seem long, you may have been dealing with a barren situation for what seems like an eternity, but please understand that great things take time to manifest. Fine wine has to be aged; gold and silver must stay in the fire for a certain amount of time for the removal of the dross, for purification. The heat you are feeling means you are moving closer to perfection, the dross is dissolving, and wilting under the fire of God. There are people who appear to be ahead of you in this life, but wait on the Lord and be of good courage. Hannah's son had to be born in God's timing because of the work that he had to do. He carried a tremendous anointing as prophet, priest and judge; maybe if Hannah had him naturally without divine intervention, she would not have dedicated him to the LORD. Perhaps if God granted your desire years ago you might not have been at the place of maturity to receive it. You may have taken another road. The things you have lacked are the things that have kept you pouring out your soul before the Lord. People do not pray for things they already have. Thank God that in the midst of your barrenness, you have drawn closer to Him.

I love the fact that 1 Samuel chapter 2 and verse 1 begins with the words, "And Hannah prayed." She started out by pouring out of her heavy soul to the LORD in her barrenness and she ends by pouring out of her soul with a joyful prayer of thanks unto the LORD.

When she left Samuel with Eli she did not go home sad, instead of melancholy she burst into a song of praise to the LORD. *"And Hannah prayed and said, My heart rejoiceth in the LORD mine horn is exalted in the LORD: my mouth is enlarged over mine enemies; because I rejoice in thy salvation" (1 Samuel 2:1).*

"Sing, O barren, thou that didst not bear; break forth into singing, and cry aloud, thou that didst not travail with child: for more are the children of the desolate than the children of the married wife, saith the LORD" (Isaiah 54:1).

There is an awesome relationship between sacrifice and song. *"And when the burnt offering began, the song of the Lord began also" (2 Chronicles 29:27).* You can not sing the song of the Lord if you have not offered the burnt offering. We are the burnt offering, the people He has tried in the fire and brought out with a song in our hearts and praise on our lips. Before Jesus went to the Mount of Olives and the garden of Gethsemane where He would be pressed like an olive so we could receive salvation and the gift of the Holy Ghost, He sang a hymn with His disciples *(Matthew 26:30).* After being humiliated and beaten Paul and Silas sang hymns to the Lord (Acts 16:20-26).

Hannah brought Samuel a new coat when the family went to Shiloh to worship the LORD. On one of their trips Eli blessed her and Elkanah and said, *"The LORD give thee seed of this woman for the loan which is lent to the LORD."* And they went unto their own home. And the LORD visited Hannah, so that she conceived, and bare three sons and two daughters.

The Lord gives seed to the sower. When we are willing to wait in prayer for His plan to be fulfilled, when we are willing to give back to the Lord that which He gave us during our barrenness, He will bring us to the place of overflow. At first she could not conceive, but after Samuel she had three more sons and two daughters. Hallelujah!!! The Prophet Isaiah declared, *"Hast thou not known? Hast thou not heard, that the everlasting God, the LORD, the Creator of the ends of the earth fainteth not, neither is weary? There is no searching of his understanding. He giveth power to the faint; and to them that have no might he increaseth strength. Even the youths shall faint and be weary, and the young men shall utterly fall: But they that wait upon the LORD shall renew their strength; they shall mount up with wings as eagles; they shall run, and not be weary; and they shall walk, and not faint" (Isaiah 40:30-31).* Our posture while waiting for deliverance at midnight should always be one of prayer and praise. We should also meditate on His word. Once we do these things there will be no room for the enemy to operate.

When God told Abram to take his beloved son Isaac to mount Moriah and offer him as a sacrifice, Abram did not stagger or faint. He demonstrated to the Lord that he was willing to part with Isaac, and God not only provided a ram in the thicket, He changed his name to Abraham which means, father of a multitude. Job lost all his children but he held fast his integrity even when his wife told him to, "curse God and die." The Lord blessed the latter end of Job more than his beginning. God gave him seven sons and three daughters. He was given ten more children. Please remember, the number ten speaks of restoration.

Ecclesiastes 3:1 To every thing there is a season, and a time to every purpose under the heaven. Your barrenness has a time appointed, it has a season. Some seasons are short and some are long. No matter how long or short your season of barrenness, please continue to pray, praise and worship. When your barrenness gives way to fruitfulness your latter days will be greater than your former. Your surroundings may be dark at the moment but hold fast to the Lord's unchanging hand because the fruit you bring forth will remain and it will bring glory to God.

EZRA PRAYED

When the Jews were given permission by King Cyrus to return to Jerusalem many of them decided to remain in Mesopotamia. Many of them were employed by the government or in business and would have had to pay a great price to relocate. Sacrifices have to be made to get to the place God is leading us. Many are stagnant spiritually because they are unwilling to make the necessary sacrifice to get to the place of divine destiny. Ezra gathered eighteen men who were the heads of Jewish families because he knew they could influence their relatives. A total of 1,515 men plus women and children agreed to go with him to Jerusalem. After traveling for a week the group stopped at the River Ahava for three days before continuing. During the three days Ezra took inventory of the people and realized there were no Levites among them. Levites are responsible for carrying the presence of the Lord on their shoulders. In this hour of darkness God is preparing the shoulders of a company of Levites who will be able to carry the Ark, His presence on their shoulders. These Levites will be able to bring the Shekinah glory, the light of the glorious gospel into dark places. Once in a while we ought to stop and take inventory to make sure our shoulders are being strengthened. We have to make sure we are carrying the presence of the Lord, because deliverance will not come to people without His presence.

Ezra sent eleven leading men to recruit some Levites for the trip and they returned with thirty eight of them. Ezra called for three days of fasting and prayer seeking God's protection for their long arduous journey. This is the crux of the whole matter. As darkness and gross darkness covers the earth and men's hearts become cold and wicked, navigating life's journey can become more difficult. We must be proactive in prayer and fasting. The purpose of the fasting and prayer according to Ezra was "to afflict themselves before God in order to seek a right way for the people, their children and for their substance." Believers have heard a lot of messages about blessings and prosperity over the years but how many people are teaching and preaching messages about the many afflictions the righteous have to suffer. I love the fact they afflicted themselves. Remember, the word afflict means *to chasten self, deal hardly with, humble,* and *to submit self.* This is not the hour or the season for the body, the church of the Lord Jesus Christ to be lusting after material things. This is not the hour for us to listen to sweet words that will entice and tickle our flesh. *"Woe unto them that call evil good, and good evil; that put darkness for light, and light for darkness; that put bitter for sweet, and sweet for bitter"* (Isaiah 5:20)! *"Woe unto them! For they have gone in the way of Cain, and ran greedily after the error of Balaam for reward, and perished in the gainsaying of Core"* (Jude 11).

We need leaders like Ezra who are going to take time out of their journey to proclaim a fast so we can afflict ourselves before our God for a better way. We do not need more man made church programs. We do not need more car washes, fish fries, or entertainment programs to raise funds. We need to get on the altar and cry out to the Lord for direction. Many in the body have lost their way because we are in the midnight hour. There is no Levite among them who have the Ark on his shoulders. Church doors are closing and pastors are leaving the ministry. Many are becoming life coaches, hooking up with secular business men and motivational speakers who they feel can instruct us how to become wealthy and influential. The body of Christ does not need worldly leaders to lead us. We need the five fold ministry to get back to teaching and preaching the apostolic doctrine of the kingdom of God. We need the apostle, the prophet, the evangelist, the pastor and the teacher, to put away their petty differences, jealousies, and insecurities, come from behind their denominational walls and work together to perfect the saints for the work of the ministry. The prosperity messages have made a select few very wealthy while many in the body are struggling to make ends meet. The hour is late; the night is upon us. Jesus said, *"I must work the works of him that sent me, while it is day: the night cometh, when no man can work."* (John 9:4).

We must be about our Father's business. His business is salvation for the lost and growth through discipleship.

The Lord knows the things we need and He will supply the need. This is the hour for us to afflict ourselves for a better way for the nations and the people who dwell therein. It is time to cry out to the Lord like Hannah, like Ezra, like the men and women in the Bible who lifted up supplication before the Lord for their nation. Hannah cried for a son who she could dedicate to the service of the Lord. Are you willing to trust God for your provision so you can spend your time crying out for young men and women who are going astray, young men and women locked up in juvenile institutions, and prisons all across the land? These are young men and women who fell by the wayside because they did not have a father like Ezra who took inventory of their situation then sat down and fasted and prayed to the God of Heaven. We can not rely on the government to alleviate the burdens of society. The church, the body of Christ must be willing to stand in the gap in this dark hour. God always has someone on the inside in times of crisis, and he has placed the church in the earth for such a time as this.

IF I PERISH I PERISH

When the Jews faced one of their midnight attacks, God had a woman on the inside named Esther. He used her to bring deliverance at a critical time in the nation's history. She was queen when wicked Haman concocted a plan to wipe out the Jews. When her cousin Mordecai heard of the plot, he "rent his clothes, and put on sackcloth with ashes, and went out into the midst of the city, and cried with a loud and bitter cry" (Esther 4:1). We need some modern day Mordecais who are willing to take off their fancy costumes and sweet smelling perfumes, put on some street clothes, get into the prisons, the crack houses, the heroin shooting galleries, and other dens of iniquity, and cry a bitter cry for the people trapped in bondage.

Esther was living in the palace as the queen while the Jews in the provinces were mourning, weeping, wailing, and fasting. Esther tried to give Mordecai a change of clothes but he refused to take it. When Mordecai told her of the decree and asked her to assist she explained that no one could go into the king without an invitation. Mordecai told her if she did not intervene then deliverance would arise from another place. When Esther heard the words of Mordecai she swung into action and told her attendants, *"Go, gather together all the Jews that are present in Shushan, and fast ye for me, and neither eat nor drink three days, night or day: I also and my maidens will fast likewise; and so will I go in unto the king, which is not according to the law: and if I perish, I perish" (Esther 4:16).* In this dark hour we need to gather with believers of like precious faith who have a desire to fast and pray. Take note of the fact she fasted the same amount of days as Ezra. The laws of the land are changing. Prayer has already been taken out of the schools and now we have young people shooting their classmates and teachers with assault weapons. The law is trying to sanction homosexual marriages while prohibiting us from publicly displaying the name of King Jesus, but we must risk life and limb to get sinners into His presence. Our declaration must be like that of Queen Esther, "If I perish, I perish."

The government needs to witness the power and the good hand of our God upon us. Ezra and the people faced a difficult trip but they knew the power and the provision of the God of their fathers. Ezra did not want to ask the king for soldiers and horsemen to protect them on their journey. They had told the king that the Hand of their God was upon those that sought Him. Ezra declared, *"For I was ashamed to require of the king a band of soldiers and horsemen to help us against the enemy in the way" (Ezra 4:22).* There is an enemy in the way of people getting saved, and delivered. His name is the devil. The only way we will defeat his demons is through the mighty hand of our God upon us.

Ezra and the people fasted and sought God for the things they needed and God honored the fasting and prayer. They went in the anointing of God. The hand of God was upon them and He delivered them from the enemies who were hiding in the way to defeat them.

When they departed from the river Ahava on the twelfth day to go to Jerusalem they had silver, gold, and vessels of fine copper for the offering of the Lord. They left the river, the place of fasting, prayer, and communing with God to go to Jerusalem, the place which means, *"Possession of peace or foundation of peace."* We have to travel through midnight to get to get to the place of peace. In our travels God will provide rivers along the way where we can rest and refresh ourselves with prayer and fasting.

NEHEMIAH PRAYED

The governor Nehemiah was a cupbearer for King Artaxerxes at the palace at Shushan in Persia. The name Nehemiah means, *"The Lord has comforted."* The position of cupbearer was one of great responsibility and privilege. At each meal he had to test the king's wine to make sure it was not poisoned. The cupbearer had great influence because of his access to the king. For almost 100 years the Jewish remnant was back in their land, but Nehemiah chose to remain at the palace. It was the right decision because God had a great work for him to do and it required him being close to the king. Nehemiah was placed by God in the position just like he placed Esther a generation before.

In the month Chisleu, in the twentieth year Nehemiah received a visit from some of the brethren from Judah. The Hebrew month

Chisleu runs from mid-November to mid-December on our calendar. Nehemiah asked his brother Hanani and the men of Judah about the Jews that had escaped the captivity and about the state of Jerusalem. Although Nehemiah had a prestigious position as the king's cupbearer he was still concerned about his people and the great city of Jerusalem. No matter how lofty the heights we climb, no matter how prestigious the position we hold in society, we must never lose concern for the people and the things of God. *"For who shall have pity upon thee, O Jerusalem? Or who shall bemoan thee? Or who shall go aside to ask how thou art" (Jeremiah 15:5)?* Jesus instructed us to "pray for the peace of Jerusalem." They told Nehemiah that the remnant were in great affliction and reproach. The wall of Jerusalem was broken down, and the gates were burned with fire. In these last and evil days the remnant of God will have to deal with great affliction. *"I went by the field of the slothful and by the vineyard of the man void of understanding; And, lo, it was all grown over with thorns, and nettles had covered the face thereof, and the stone wall thereof was broken down. Then I saw, and considered it well: I looked upon it, and received instruction. Yet a little sleep, a little slumber, a little folding of the hands to sleep: So shall thy poverty come as one that of a robber; and thy want as an armed man" (Proverbs 24:31-34).* The fact that the wall of Jerusalem was broken down meant they were exposed to bandits. Solomon said, Jerusalem was the most important city in Israel, a city beloved by its people and a fortified wall was important for protection. Concerning Jerusalem the Jews that were held captive in Babylon said, *"If I forget thee, O Jerusalem, let my right hand forget her cunning. If I do not remember thee, let my tongue cleave to the roof of my mouth; if I prefer not Jerusalem above my chief joy" (Psalm 137:5-6).*

When Nehemiah received the report concerning the remnant and the city of Jerusalem he did not panic. He sat down and wept, mourned, fasted, and prayed. It was a midnight situation for him and his response gives us an understanding why his name means the Lord has comforted. When you are in the midst of your midnight situation do not allow emotions to cause you to make decisions that will worsen matters. You will have times of despair and melancholy but your first response has to be fasting and prayer. Nehemiah prayed day and night before the God of heaven. There are twelve instances in the book of Nehemiah where he prayed. The book opens and closes with prayer. He confessed his sin and the sin of the people. He did not exclude himself when he asked God to forgive the people's sin. He knew that sin was the thing that led to the captivity and the destruction of Jerusalem. When praying for deliverance from a midnight situation the first thing to do is to ask for forgiveness of sins. *If my people, which are called by my name, shall humble themselves, and pray, and seek my face, and turn from their wicked ways; then will I hear from heaven, and will forgive their sin, and will heal their land. (2 Chronicles 7:14)*

Nehemiah was a true intercessor. He stood in the gap and lifted up supplication unto the Lord at a dark time in the nation's history. Four months later in the month Nisan, the king noticed the sad countenance of Nehemiah as he took up the wine and gave it to the king. A cupbearer's life could be in jeopardy if his countenance was sad before the king. This is the first time that he appeared before the king with a sad countenance, so it tells us how deeply he carried the burden. He was very afraid when the king asked him why his countenance was sad. He explained to the king that his sadness was due to the condition his fathers' sepulchers and the gates that were consumed with fire. When the king inquired about what he needed his response was to pray to the God of heaven. Every major decision made by the children of God should be prefaced by prayer. Prayer was important for Nehemiah because he needed God to touch the heart of the king. He needed the king's permission, he needed the king's provision, and he needed the king's protection. Nehemiah knew the heart of the king was in the hands of God.

After praying he told the king, *"If it please the king, and if thy servant have found favour in thy sight that thou wouldest send me unto Judah, unto the city of my fathers' sepulchers, that I may build it"* (Nehemiah 2: 5). It pleased the king to send Nehemiah; when we have a consistent prayer life we will please the king and obtain favor. He was given everything he needed for the building project.

Our Lord and Savior Jesus Christ is the Word that became flesh and dwelt among men. Although He was the Son of God and had the Holy Ghost without measure he had an active and vibrant prayer life. *"And it came to pass in those days, that he went out into a mountain to pray, and continued all night in prayer to God" (Luke 6:12).* If our Lord thought it necessary to pray fervently then we must make sure we pray fervently. The disciples understood the importance of prayer and that is evidenced by the fact they asked Jesus to teach them to pray as John taught his disciples. If we develop our prayer life, prayer will come naturally when the midnight hour is upon us.

PRAYING WOMEN

Prior to encountering the young lady at Philippi who was used by her masters for fortune telling, Paul and Silas had an encounter with some praying women. That encounter opened the door for the first church on the continent of Europe. *"And a vision appeared to Paul in the night; There stood a man of Macedonia, and prayed him, saying, Come over into Macedonia, and help us" (Acts 16:9).* After receiving the vision The Apostle traveled to Philippi which was a chief city of Macedonia. His custom upon entering a new city was to find the synagogue and preach Christ. The Jewish population may have been small in Philippi because there was no synagogue there. Ten Jewish males were required to have a synagogue in a city. There were arches at the entrance of the city of Philippi with an inscription forbidding foreign religions.

Paul and Silas abided in the city several days until they found out about a prayer meeting conducted by a group of women by the river on the Sabbath. It is ironic that Paul had seen a man in the vision at Troas but it would be a group of women that were praying by the river. The Bible exposition commentary on the New Testament states, "It is better that the words of the Law be burned than be delivered to a woman!" Paul was a convert to Jesus Christ and was no longer operating as a Pharisee so he had no problem ministering to the women. Lydia was a successful business woman from the city of Thyatira who had made her fortune selling purple dye. The Bible describes Lydia as someone who worshipped God. It also says "The Lord opened her heart." Worship opens doors, gates, windows and hearts. When an individual is willing to worship the Lord He will manifest Glory in his life. When Lydia heard Paul share the Gospel she received the Word of the Lord and was baptized. So were all the people in her household. She opened her house to the Apostle and the first church meetings on the continent of Europe were held in her home. Thank God for praying women; thank God for men of God like Paul and Silas who refuse to discriminate against women because of their gender.

Chapter 3
MIDNIGHT: THE TIME TO IMPORTUNE

THE PRAYER OF IMPORTUNITY

Several years ago, the Lord began to deal with me about my prayer life. At the time my prayer life was very anemic. I did not have an active prayer life and the Lord impressed upon me the need to spend more time not only in prayer but in fasting. He said it was not enough just to be able to preach and teach the Word. I had to develop a dedicated prayer life for where He was taking me and what He wanted to do in and through me. Spiritual warfare cannot be fought effectively if the child of Christ does not have a dedicated prayer life. I believe we have to have a life of proactive prayer. What I mean by proactive prayer is we should not wait for tragedy to befall us or our loved ones before we fast and pray.

I felt the need to rise early in the morning and dedicate the first couple hours of my day to intercessory prayer. I began to meditate on the Words Jesus spoke when He told His disciples that, "Men ought always to pray, and not to faint." (Luke 18:1). The Greek word for faint is egkakeo (pronounced eng-kak-eh-o), and it means to be afraid, to become discouraged, and to lose heart. Prayer keeps us in constant communication with our Father and we will go from weakness to strength once we remain connected to Him. Although Jesus told His disciples that men ought always to pray and not to faint, He went on to tell them about a widow that kept appearing before an unjust judge. Jesus was teaching His disciples about the importance of persistent prayer. We have to learn to pray persistently and consistently because the answers to our prayers might take some time to manifest. If we are not tenacious we might want to give up in the midnight hour. The widow wanted the judge to avenge her of her adversary but he would not. The woman refused to quit and kept appearing in his courtroom with her petition. Jesus tells the parable to let the believer know that she should not give up if her prayers are not answered right away. She must continue to be tenacious like the widow. The widow was so persistent in her pursuit of justice that the judge finally said, *"Though I fear not God, nor regard man; yet because this widow troubleth me, I will revenge her, lest by her continual coming she weary me."* That phrase literally means, *"Lest she give me a black eye."*

PERSISTENCE PAYS

Allow me to share a wonderful story on persistence I received from a friend.

It is the great equalizer for all of those reaching for success. It overcomes lack of education, money, talent, intelligence, looks and all other seemingly advantageous things. President Calvin Coolidge said nothing could take its place.

"Persistence and determination alone are omnipotent."

I cannot think of one victory I've ever had that I won without persistence. For a while I just thought that I had to work harder and longer than anyone else in order to achieve because nothing has ever come easy for me. Then I really looked around and noticed that everyone else was just like me. Every mentor I've ever had and every successful person I've ever known has their own story of how persistence was the key to their success.

One of the greatest Universal Laws is called the Law of Gender: "This law decrees that all seeds (ideas are spiritual seeds) have a gestation or incubation period before they manifest. In other words, when you choose a goal or build the image in your mind, a definite period of time must elapse before that image manifests in physical results."

Knowing the basics of farming I certainly understand the gestation of a seed. In fact, one of my most favorite inspirational examples about persistence is the story of an Asian Bamboo species that even after five years of watering, weeding and fertilizing is barely visible. Then in a span of about six weeks it grows two and a half feet a day to 90 feet and higher. It grows so fast that you can literally "hear" it growing. The question to ask is did the bamboo grow 90 feet in six weeks or did it grow 90 feet in five years? Obviously it grew 90 feet in five years, for all the time when growth was not visible it was developing a massive root system that would later supports magnificent growth.

Can you see where the current circumstances in your life are developing your massive root system? Can you see where you must continue to "fertilize" and "water" yourself even though maybe you cannot see any visible changes today?

Napoleon Hill thought that persistence was such a key to success that he devoted an entire chapter to it in the classic Think and Grow Rich. He writes, "Persistence is a state of mind, therefore it can be cultivated. Before success comes in any person's life, he is sure to meet with much temporary defeat, and, perhaps, some failure. When defeat overtakes a person, the easiest and most logical thing to do is to QUIT."

That is exactly what the majority of people do. More than five hundred of the most successful people this country has ever known told the author their greatest success came one step beyond the point at which defeat had overtaken them.

Mr. Chad Schapiro

When we are faced with a midnight situation we cannot allow ourselves to fall into a pity party. That is the time we must find the inner strength to press in prayer, to bombard the Heavens until an answer is released. We must be patient and persistent, remember that the demonic realm does not want us to receive the answer to our prayers. During a twenty day fast, Daniel was told by the Angel Gabriel, "From the first day that thou didst set thine heart to understand, and to chasten thyself before thy God, thy words were heard, and I am come for thy words. But the prince of the kingdom of

Persia withstood me one and twenty days: but lo, Michael, one of the chief princes, came to help me; and I remained there with the kings of Persia" (Daniel 10:12-13). In Daniel's case the answer was released right away but the Angel had to battle demons to get the answer to Daniel. With this story in mind we must realize that the enemy is going to do everything he can to stop us from receiving our answer. There are times where we will have to pray for a loved one trapped in a midnight situation, and we might have to pray for years. We must be careful not to despair or become despondent if the answer does not come right away.

Daniel's midnight was captivity and a Lion's den but he never lost his consistency in prayer. You might have to pray from a difficult place but whatever the environment, please do not stop praying. The devil will try to turn up the heat on us in an attempt to get us to abandon our prayer life but we must endeavor to stay connected to God in prayer, especially in the midnight hour. When the king signed a decree stating that anyone praying to another God would be thrown into the Lion's den, Daniel kept on praying to his God. The Bible says, *"Now when Daniel knew that the writing was signed, he went into his house; and his windows being open in his chamber toward Jerusalem, he kneeled upon his knees three times a day, and prayed, and gave thanks before his God, as he did aforetime" (Daniel 6:10).* Jerusalem means "possession of peace or foundation of peace" and was considered the city of God. Daniel had peace at the prospect of being fed to the lions because he stayed connected to the place and God of peace. He knew there was no distance in prayer. Prayer can reach places we are not able to go and accomplish things we are not able to accomplish.

When you are praying in the night hour there are times when you will be alone because the people around you will not be able to go the distance. Jesus experienced that when He and His disciples were in the Garden of Gethsemane. Gethsemane means oil press and Jesus was being pressed under the weight of the road that lay ahead. All he asked his disciples to do was to sit and watch while he went and prayed. Unfortunately they fell asleep and were not able to watch with him for one hour. When the midnight hour comes, will you slumber and sleep when you are supposed to be watching? The word watch in Greek is gregoreuo (pronounced gray-gor-yoo-o), and it means to keep awake, to be vigilant. Jesus told His disciples to watch and pray, so they would not enter into temptation because the spirit is willing, but the flesh is weak. The Apostle Peter said believers should be sober and vigilant because our adversary the devil, as a roaring, lion walketh about, seeking whom he may devour. The Greek word for vigilant is the same word used by Jesus when He told His disciples to watch. The Greek word for devour is *katapino* and it means to drink down, to drown or to swallow. The devil wants to consume us so we must be watchful and sober. The Greek word for sober is *nepho* (pronounced nay-fo) and it does not only mean to abstain from wine, it also means to watch, and to be discreet.

When lions are hunting they survey the pack of animals they are about to attack in-order to identify the weak one. Once the weak one is identified they will swarm that animal and kill it. Without a consistent and persistent prayer life, a believer will become faint and fall prey to the devices of the devil. If we do not pray then we will become prey. The book of Job backs up the Apostle Peter's statement that the devil is walking about like a roaring lion seeking whom he may devour. *"Now there was a day when the sons of God came to present themselves before the Lord, and Satan came also among them. And the Lord said unto Satan, whence comest thou? Then Satan answered the Lord and said, from going to and fro in the earth, and from walking up and down in it" (Job 1:6-7).* Satan was not walking to and fro, up and down the earth because he needed to burn some calories. He was looking for believers to devour. The Lord pointed out Job to the devil because Job was a mature believer and God knew he could handle the attack. It is not a matter of if but when we will have to face a midnight situation so it behooves us to be grounded in prayer. Job asked the question *"Is it fit to say to a king, thou art wicked? And to princes, ye are ungodly? How much less to him that accepteth not the persons of princes, nor regarded the rich more than the poor? For they all are the work of his hands. In a moment shall they die, and the people shall be troubled at midnight, and pass away: and the mighty shall be taken away without hand" (Job 34:20).* A persistent prayer life prepares the believer for the trouble that arrives at midnight. Once we are anchored in prayer the midnight trouble will not be able to dislodge us and cause us to drift into an abyss of despair and degradation.

During one of His personal prayer times Jesus' disciples came to Him and requested He teach them to pray like John taught his disciples. We know that prayer is simply communicating with our heavenly Father, but the disciples request lets us know there are certain aspects of prayer that have to be taught. Jesus taught them what we commonly call "the Lord's Prayer." After teaching them this model for prayer He asked them a question. "Which of you shall have a friend, and shall go unto him at midnight, and say unto him, Friend, lend me three loaves; For a friend of mine in his journey is come to me, and I have nothing to set before him? The visit by the friend did not happen at an opportune time; on the contrary the visit was at an inopportune time because in those days people did not open their doors at night because of fear of robbers. The writer is careful to let us know that it is not just night but midnight. The time that the person went to his friend is an indication that his need was urgent.

The word "lend" as it is used here does not mean borrowing with the intention to pay back. It comes from the Greek word *chraomai* (pronounced khrah-om-ahee) which means to furnish what is needed. Although the hour was not favorable I am sure the man felt his request would be granted because he was asking a friend and he only needed three loaves. The man had nothing to set before his friend who traveled a long way to visit him. In that culture it was embarrassing not to have refreshments when visited by a friend. The friend would not rise and give him because his door was shut and he and his family were in bed. We have an expectation that our friends will go the distance for us in our time of greatest need. When I was younger I heard people say, "a friend in need is a friend in deed." You will know who your true friends are when you arrive at their door with an urgent request at midnight.

Midnight is a time when it appears that all doors are shut and you cannot get a break from family and friends because they are dealing with their own trials. The open and shut door is a principle in the scriptures. Concerning prayer Jesus said, *"But thou, when thou prayest, enter into thy closet, and when thou hast shut thy door, pray to thy Father which is in secret; and thy Father which seeth in secret shall reward thee openly" (Matthew 6:6).* In the Book of Revelation the Apostle John wrote, *"After this I looked, and, behold, a door was opened in heaven: and the first voice which I heard was as it were of a trumpet talking with me; which said, Come up hither, and I will show thee things which must be hereafter" (Revelation 4:1).* Persistent prayer opens doors in Heaven and gives us sensitivity to the voice of the Lord. John was not vacationing at some resort when he heard the voice of a trumpet beckoning him to "come up hither." He was on an island called Patmos, and Patmos means "my killing." Revelation 1:9 tells us why John was there. "I John, who also am your brother, and companion in tribulation, and in the kingdom and patience of Jesus Christ, was in the isle that is called Patmos, for the word of God, and for the testimony of Jesus Christ. Midnight situations will kill the flesh in preparation for hearing what God has to say to us. There cannot be a testimony without a test; the greater the test, the greater the testimony. We are not going to get happy meal trials for steak and lobster blessings. The amount of revelation you walk in will be commensurate with the amount of trials you have to endure.

John refused to allow his banishment to the island of Patmos to hinder his flow in the Spirit. Though he was banished he was able to say, "I was in the Spirit on the Lord's day." Refuse to allow your environment or the darkness of your situation to keep your from going higher in the realm of the Spirit. Doors might be shut for you now but you are just a prayer and praise away from experiencing open doors of blessings. It will take effectual fervent prayer and the type of radical praise Paul and Silas gave at midnight to see the dark situations give way to light.

Concerning the man that went to his friend to borrow the three loaves Jesus said, *"Though he will not rise and give him, because he is his friend, yet because of his importunity he will rise and give him as many as he needeth" (Luke 11:5).* Some people will not give us the things we need just because of friendship. There is a gospel song that has lyrics stating, "I am a friend of God." It is awesome and wonderful to be a friend of God, but we have to understand the dynamics of the friendship. God will not hand things to us because we are friends of His. The Lord is saying we have to have a certain posture in prayer if we are to receive from Him. That posture has to be fervency. If you can catch the revelation of the **Prayer of Importunity** then you can get your breakthrough at midnight like Paul and Silas did; you can get more than the three loaves like the individual who came to his friend at midnight requesting the bread. After explaining to His disciples that the man received all the bread he needed, not because he was a friend but because of his importunity, Jesus went on to say, *"Ask, and it shall be given you; seek, and ye shall find; knock, and it shall be opened unto you. For every one that asketh receiveth; and he that seeketh findeth; and to him that knocketh it shall be opened"* *(Luke 11:9-10).*

On the surface it appears Jesus is saying that all we have to do is ask, seek, and knock and we will receive, find, and doors will be opened unto us but the revelation or the key is how we ask, how we seek, and how we knock. This is where importunity comes in. Importunity is the key to receiving what we are asking, seeking, and knocking for. Random House Webster's Collegiate Dictionary defines the word importune as, "To urge or press with excessive persistence; to make urgent or persistent solicitations. In the Greek it conveys the idea of "urgency, audacity, and boldness." Believers who know how to press in prayer and praise in the midnight hour will receive the things they desire, find the things they are looking for and have doors opened unto them in the realm of the spirit. If we hand our children everything they ask for we will encourage them to be lazy and slothful. God adopts the same principle with us. He withholds things from us so we can learn to fight the good fight of faith, so we learn to pray without ceasing.

If God handed us everything we asked for we would not pray as we should. God knows there will be midnight situations that His children will have to face and if we are not battle tested we will not gain the victory. Paul and Silas were battle tested in prayer and praise, so when midnight came in the inner prison instead of having a pity party they had a prayer and praise celebration. They understood the prayer of importunity. It takes discipline to get to a place where you can pray and praise at midnight. The prayer and praise posture you adopt before midnight will determine how you conduct yourself at midnight when you have to walk by faith and not by sight. At midnight you will not be able to rely on natural ability because the situation will be extremely dark. You will have to dig deep to draw from the prayer and praise God has perfected in you by reason of use. Instead of murmuring and complaining about the midnight situation you are dealing with at the present time; use it as an opportunity to press in prayer with excessive force. We have to learn to go higher and there are times when the adversity we face at midnight is the thing that forces us to muster the strength to climb higher.

CHILDREN OBEY YOUR PARENTS IN THE LORD

"Children are a heritage of the LORD: and the fruit of the womb is his reward" (Psalm 127:3). I never fully comprehended the sacrifices my parents made for me until I started having children of my own. When I struggle to pay a light bill I can remember the days when my mom repeatedly told me to "turn off the lights when I was not using them." When I struggle to put food on the table for my own children I remember the times I fed the food I did not like to our dog. I remember the times I threw good food in the garbage, not thinking about the fact my mom had to work hard to provide it. Children are a heritage and the fruit of the womb but they can be a pain in the posterior at times. When you are young and strong you feel there is not much anyone can tell you. There are many things my mother told me that I disregarded only to see them come to fruition. Listening to the wisdom of parents gained through trial and error can help us avoid many of the pitfalls of midnight.

Samson was a Nazarite, a product of prayer who was born to be a deliverer of his people. Nazarite means "separated one." According to Numbers six, a Nazarite was never to drink strong drink or touch a dead body. When his barren mother received a visitation from the angel of the LORD informing her she would conceive and bear a son, the angel instructed her that her Son should not drink wine or strong drink; he should not eat any unclean thing, no razor should touch his head. His uncut hair would be a mark of his dedication to the LORD. He was to be a Nazarite from the womb to the day of his death. When she told her husband about the visitation, he entreated the LORD. He prayed and asked God to send the angel to them again so he could teach them how to bring up the child. When Samson was born the LORD blessed him, and he was moved by the Spirit of the

LORD. The Bible says, *"And the spirit of the LORD began to move him at times in the camp of Dan between Zorah and Eshtaol."* Zorah was a town in the low country of Judah; the name Zorah means place of wasps. Eshtaol means narrow pass or recess, and it was also a town in the low country of Judah. It is the narrow road which leads to salvation. Samson was born to travel some narrow roads which meant he would have to rely on the LORD to protect him from the sting of wasps.

He was blessed by the Lord with great strength but he got to the point where he started to rely on his strength instead of the source of the strength. As he grew in strength, he began to defy his parents. Young people need to understand that many of them are products of prayer and should honor their mothers and fathers so their days can be longer on this earth. Judges chapter 14 verses 1 and 2 begin with statements which epitomize the life of Samson. Judges 14:1 begins with the words, "And Samson went down," while verse 2 begins with the statement, "And he came up." In many instances the way up is down, the way to become rich is to become poor, and the way to live is to learn to die; It is all dependent on the places you go down to, the type of riches you desire and what you seek to do with those riches, and whether or not the life you want to live is one of reverence for God. As we will see, Samson went down to places he should not have gone to, did things he should not have done, and lost his life in a way that I believe, he should not have.

Samson went down to Timnath and saw one of the daughters of the Philistines and told his parents to get her so he could marry her. The Philistines were the enemy of Israel and had dominion over them because of their rebellion against God. Samson's desire to go down to Timnath was of the LORD because it gave him the provocation he needed to fight against the Philistines. But while he was there he did something to break the Nazarite vow. A young lion roared against Samson when he was by the vineyards of Timnath. The roaring of the Lion should have been a wake up call. As a Nazarite he was not supposed to drink from the fruit of the vine.

The fact that he was at the vineyard of Timnath was a sign of danger. Lion is a symbol of kingship, royalty, courage and boldness of good and evil persons. It is important to note that the text declares it was a young lion meaning it was not mature enough to overcome Samson, because the Spirit of the LORD was with him. But the roar should have been a warning to him to walk circumspect. He was born in the narrow place of wasps and now he is by the vineyards of Timnath hearing the roar of a young lion. The Spirit of the LORD came upon him mightily and he was able to tear the lion apart with his hands. The Spirit of the LORD strengthens us and gives us the ability to deal with our adversaries but we must never forget that our strength comes from the Spirit of the LORD and not from our innate ability. For this reason God says, *"Not by might, nor by power, but by my spirit, saith the LORD" (Zechariah 4:6).* We will be mighty and powerful against our foes when we yield to the Spirit of the LORD and not to our own strength.

On page 103 of her book, The Peace & Power of Knowing God's Name, Author Kay Arthur writes, *"There are times when you look around you and your first response is despair. The odds against you seem overwhelming. The situation in which you find yourself seems unbearable. The forces arrayed against you seem overpowering. You are overmatched, and you know it. You are at the very end of your strength, and you feel it. You are in deep trouble, and you sense defeat and darkness closing in on all sides. O Beloved, there is a name you may call upon in times of conflict and warfare. It is a name that makes the very pillars of the universe tremble. Jehovah-sabaoth-The Lord of Hosts. "*

Samson did not share the defeat of the young lion with his parents. We should endeavor to share with our spiritual parents the victories we gain over spiritual lions because after great spiritual victories come great spiritual attacks. After defeating the prophets of Baal the Prophet Elijah fled from Jezebel and hid in a cave. After defeating the young lion Samson went down and spoke to the woman of Timnath, and she pleased him. On a return trip to see her, the Bible declares, *"And after a time he returned to take her, and he turned aside to see the carcass of the lion: and, behold, there was a swarm of bees and honey in the carcass of the lion. And he took thereof in his hands, and went on eating, and came to his father and mother, and he gave them, and they did eat: but he told not them that he had taken the honey of the carcass of the lion" (Judges 14:8-9).* Beloved, be careful what people are feeding you because some things that are sweet to the taste are bitter to the stomach. As a Nazarite, Samson was not to touch the unclean dead carcass of the lion much less to eat from it. When we make a vow to serve the Lord in the beauty of holiness we must keep our eyes focused on Him and do our best to keep our vows. There will be things that will entice us and tempt us to turn aside but we must endeavor to stay focused and to keep our eyes on the prize. Ladies and Gentlemen, It does not matter how cute or sweet the honey is, it will cause problems if it comes from some dead thing the Lord has told us not to touch.

Samson's father in-law gave Samson's wife to another man. Samson was so furious that his father in-law did this that he burned the corn fields, the vineyards, and the olives of the Philistines. When the Philistines found out that Samson destroyed their fields they burned his wife and her father. Disobedience often starts out small but if left unchecked it will grow until the parties involved are consumed. Samson slaughtered the Philistines to avenge the death of his wife. The Philistines went up and pitched in Judah. Judah is praise and praise should always go up. They pitched in Judah in hopes of binding Samson. Judah is our strength because praise is our strength. The enemy will always attempt to bind our praise. He will do any and everything to come up against Judah because if he binds our praise he can weaken us. When Nehemiah and the people were rebuilding the wall, enemies conspired against them. *"Nevertheless we made our prayer unto our God, and set a watch against them day and night, because of them. And Judah said, The strength of the bearers of burdens is decayed, and there is much rubbish; so that we are not able to build the wall. And our adversaries said, they shall not know, neither see, till we come in the midst among them, and slay them, and cause the work to cease" (Nehemiah 4:9-11).* If the enemy can stop Judah he can sneak in and hinder the work God has called us to do.

The men of Judah were so fearful of the Philistines they wanted to bind Samson in-order to turn him over to them. What a sad state of affairs. Praise is a weapon that should be used against the enemy. We must not allow a spirit of fear to aid the enemy in using our own weapon against us. They bound Samson with two new cords and brought him up from the rock. Two is the number of witness and separation. They used new cords because they knew how strong he was and did not want to risk breakage from old cords. The only way we can keep the enemy from binding us is to stay on the Solid Rock. Hallelujah!!! When the Philistines came against him the Spirit of the LORD came upon him mightily and the cords were loosed off his hands, Samson was able to defeat a thousand Philistines with the jaw bone of an ass. After the battle he was very thirsty and cried out to the LORD and said, *"Thou has given this great deliverance into the hand of thy servant: and now shall I die for thirst, and fall into the hand of the uncircumcised" (Judges 15:18).* Water is symbolic of the Holy Spirit and Samson's thirst was an indication that he was not relying on the strength of the Spirit of the LORD. Verse 19 begins with the words "But God." Beloved, when your situation appears to be darkest, when your health, your marriage, your finances appear to be at their lowest, please do not say God but. Instead, say "But God will shine his light, But God will heal my body, But God will restore my marriage, But God will be Jehovah Jireh the LORD who provides for me." The Jaw is a symbol of strength, and power. (Isaiah 30:28, Judges 15:16; Job 29:17; Ezekiel 29:4)

When the Nation of Israel needed water in the desert God allowed Moses to get water from the rock. There is a hollow place of strength in God where we can receive water when we are thirsty. The cisterns of religion and that of the world cannot quench our thirst, only Jesus the Solid Rock can fill our bellies with rivers of living water.

DO NOT BE COMPLACENT IN VICTORY

Human beings are creatures of habit and we tend to rely heavily on the things that are working for us. I know there is an adage which says, 'if it ain't broke don't fix it,' but once in awhile it is good to check to make sure there is no unseen breakage in the things we use. Samson was accustomed to defeating the Philistines so he figured every time they attacked he would be able to overcome them. When the enemy sees that one methodology is not effective he will try another.

Samson took unnecessary risks because he felt his strength could get him out of any situation he found himself in. His arrogance caused him to go to places and get involved with people he should have stayed clear of. Whenever he dealt with the Philistines he always went down but when he went to his father's house he always went up. Judges 16 says he went to Gaza, and saw a harlot, and went unto her. No man should join himself to a harlot and a Nazarite should not go in unto a harlot. A Nazarite took a vow to keep himself chaste and pure before the Lord. According to Genesis 38 Judah's daughter in-law Tamar covered herself with a veil and sat in an open place which was by the way to Timnath because she was a widow and Judah did not give her to be wed to his son Shelah. *"When Judah saw her, he thought her to be an harlot; because she had covered her face" (Genesis 38:15).* Judah turned unto her because he did not know it was his daughter in-law. We have to be careful of the turns we make. When we take our eyes off Godly things to look at things that are pleasing to the flesh, trouble is lurking in the background. She made Judah give her a pledge which consisted of his signet, his bracelets, and his staff. A signet is a seal, especially one used officially to mark documents. It is a way of endorsing something. A staff is a symbol of strength and guidance. A bracelet is a symbol of betrothal or a pledge.

The brother of the prodigal son told his father that his younger son had devoured his substance with harlots. One of the things the father told the servants to put on the younger son to restore him was a ring on his hand. Judah was willing to give his seal of authority, his symbol of strength, and his symbol of betrothal to someone he thought was a harlot.

The Lord honored Samson's parents by blessing Samson with the strength to defeat his enemies but he took it for granted. Samson had no business going in to the harlot at Gaza. The trip to Gaza meant Samson was going deeper into enemy territory to satisfy his craving for the heathen Philistine women. I can honestly look back on my own life and say there are some places I have gone to see women and those places were very dangerous. Samson was on a slippery slope to destruction and refused to heed the warning signs. The word Gaza is from a root word which means strong, harsh, fierce, greedy, and mighty. When the Gazites found out Samson was in the neighborhood, they surrounded the house in which he stayed. The Bible says, *"They compassed him in, and laid wait for him all night in the gate of the city, and were quiet all the night, saying, in the morning, when it is day, we shall kill him" (Judges 16:1-2).* When we take the blessings of God for granted by not being diligent in prayer and praise we will be oblivious to enemies lying quietly in the night waiting for the morning to destroy us.

"And Samson lay till midnight, and arose at midnight, and took the doors of the gate of the city, and the two posts, and went away with them, bar and all, and put them upon his shoulders, and carried them up to the top of an hill that is before Hebron" (Judges 16:3). Samson was smart enough to arise at midnight instead of the morning and was able to escape his enemies but it only made him trust in his strength more and cause him to indulge in reckless behavior.

And it came to pass afterward, that he loved a woman in the valley of Sorek, whose name was Delilah" (Judges 16:4). The word *Sorek* means *vine* and as a Nazarite Samson was not supposed to consume the intoxicating wine from the vine of the harlot in Sorek. He was entering the valley of decision where the intoxicating fragrance of the Harlot Delilah would cause his knees to buckle. The name Delilah means languishing and this woman that Samson languished with in the valley of Sorek would be the one that caused his demise. The Lords of the Philistines bribed her to entice Samson in-order to learn the source of his immense strength. The Hebrew word for entice is *pathah* and it means *to allure, to deceive, to flatter* or *to persuade.* James 1:13-15 declares, *"Let no man say when he is tempted, I am tempted of God: for God cannot be tempted with evil, neither tempteth he any man: But every man is tempted, when he is drawn away of his own lust, and enticed. Then when lust hath conceived, it bringeth forth sin: and sin, when it is finished, bringeth for death."* The stronghold of lust has brought down many great men and women.

Delilah was persistent in her desire to obtain the secret of Samson's strength. She tried three times to no avail and with each failure Samson toyed with her and the Philistines who surrounded her house. The enemy takes no vacation when it comes to his desire to destroy the people of God. Delilah kept pressing him. The Bible says *"she pressed him daily with her words, and urged him, so that his soul was vexed unto death."* She wore down his defenses until he told her all his heart. *Proverbs 7:21-27 declares, "With her much fair speech she caused him to yield, with the flattering of her lips she forced him. He goeth after her straightway, as an ox goeth to the slaughter, or as a fool to the correction of the stocks; Till a dart strike through his liver; as a bird hasteth to the snare, and knoweth not that it is for his life. Hearken unto me now therefore, O ye children, and attend to the words of my mouth. Let not thine heart decline to her ways, go not astray in her paths. For she hath cast down many wounded: yea, many strong men have been slain by her. Her house is the way to hell, going down to the chambers of death."*

It is always best not to lay with harlots, but if you rebel and do so, please do not reveal all your heart. Anything you say can and will be used against you. She rocked Samson to sleep on her knees and then she sent for the lords of the philistines. Notice she did not send for any Philistine but the lords of the Philistines. When there is a great calling on your life you will be attacked by high ranking demons. While he was sleeping she sent for a man and had him shave the seven locks of his head. Men of God have no business falling asleep in the house of a harlot and definitely should not have their head in her lap. The Apostle John had his head in the bosom of Jesus, and that is the place where we should be resting. Jesus told the disciples to, "watch and pray that ye enter not into temptation for the spirit is willing but the flesh is weak." Hair is the symbol of man's glory. It is also a type of covering; by cutting the seven locks she completely neutralized him because seven is the number of completion. Once he was neutralized she started afflicting him. Many men leave their wives because they are enticed by a harlot and as soon as she puts the hook in him she will afflict him. When the ex-wife sees him she can see the pathetic wimp he has become.

Samson's lack of prayer and praise at midnight and his trust in his own strength dulled his discernment and caused him to be overpowered by a spirit of lust. The mighty man of God was reduced to a weak man being afflicted by a harlot. The Hebrew word for afflict is, *anah.* It means to *look down,* to *browbeat,* to *depress,* to *defile,* and to *weaken.* It was a triumph for Delilah and the Philistines because Samson was their nemesis. The Bible admonishes us to be strong in the Lord and the power of His might, but that does not mean we can go anywhere and do any thing. Sin will take us to places we should not go, keep us longer than we need to stay and cost us more than we need to pay. Samson was sleeping with the enemy and it would cost him his vision. Without a vision a person will perish.

When he woke up and realized the Philistines were upon him his response was, "I will go out as at other times before, and shake myself. And he wist not that the LORD was departed from him." What a sad condition for the man of God to be in. He was so detached from the things of God that he did not realize that the LORD had departed from him. Samson thought he would do what he always did, but man-made religious traditions will not sustain us in the midnight hour. We have to be sensitive to the moving of the Holy Ghost and be willing to change. There was no mention of God or a desire to call upon the LORD for deliverance from his enemies. There was no prayer or praise, just a reliance on his strength.

The first thing the Philistines did was blind his eyes. Eyes speak of vision or light. After blinding him they brought him down to Gaza, bound him with fetters of brass, and made him grind in the prison house. Brass is a symbol of judgment against sin, strength, endurance. (Revelation 1:15 Job 40:18; Leviticus 26:19) What a terrible way for the man of God to end up. Instead of being on the battlefield Samson is in the camp of the enemy grinding corn. He became a laughingstock of the Philistines. They gave all the glory to their fish-god Dagon.

God is a God of mercy and grace and at some point Samson's hair began to grow again. A brother in Christ shared with me an awesome revelation he heard. He told me "the Philistines cut his hair but they did not kill the root." There may be some things that have been cut off from you but you will begin to grow again because you are planted in Jesus and you have a strong root system. My God!!! You might be dealing with the weakness of a midnight situation like a lengthy prison sentence, because you failed to heed the many warnings God sent your way. But I am here to tell you your strength will be replenished if you turn and cry out to God. You may have hooked up with some harlot who enticed you and caused you to languish on her lap then turned and set you up. Now you are the laughingstock but do not lose hope because the Bible declares that, *"the hair of his head began to grow again."* We cannot play the blame game when we have taken a course of action that has led us to the poor house or the prison house. We must take responsibility for our actions and repent; once we repent God will start the restoration process. The restoration process does not mean that the prison doors will open immediately although there is nothing impossible with God. The restoration process means God has forgiven you and will set things in motion for your comeback.

With the growth of Samson's hair, his strength returned. The Philistines decided to make a sport out of Samson when they needed to be entertained. With the aid of a lad Samson was able to find the pillars that held up the house where the Philistines had gathered. When you are in a dark and desolate place just find the foundation or the pillars of that place and use your prayer and praise as a weapon to shake the foundations. In previous battles Samson was able to escape because he was stronger than all his attackers. But now he had been weakened because Delilah shaved his head, and he had not fully recovered because he was blind and his hair was just beginning to grow. Samson was in a place and a state where he had to rely on someone else. First it was the lad who led him to the pillars of the house, and then Samson did something we did not see him do before. The Bible says, *"And Samson called unto the LORD, and said, O Lord God, Remember me, I pray thee, and strengthen me, I pray thee, only this once, O God, that I may be at once avenged of the Philistines for my two eyes" (Judges 16:28).* In the midnight hour when we are compassed with darkness and the enemy is mocking us we only need to cry out in prayer to our God and say, "O Lord remember me, I pray thee, and strengthen me." He will hear us and avenge us. Do not allow pride to cause you to die in your condition.

Pride comes before the fall and a haughty spirit before destruction. Cry out to the LORD in a prayer of repentance. Samson had praying parents but we find only two instances where he prayed, once for water when he was thirsty and for strength to destroy the Philistines. Prayer is great in times of calamity but we cannot afford to wait until the midnight hour of crisis to pray. We have to pray without ceasing in preparation for dealing with the crisis before it comes upon us. He asked God to strengthen him once more so he could avenge himself of the Philistines. He took hold of the two middle pillars which held up the house, one in his right hand and one in his left. The Bible declares that Samson's last words were, "Let me die with the Philistines." We do not need God's strength to die we need his strength to live. Our cry should be, "Lord let me live in your presence." Samson's brethren took his body and buried it "between Zorah and Eshtaol"- the very place where his ministry started.

Samson's desire for Philistine women led to his demise. He had great physical strength but had a weakness of lust in the flesh. A chain is only as strong as its weakest link and no matter how strong we are we must ask God to deliver us from areas where we are weak. Our greatest foe is not the enemy it is the inner-me. It is the propensity and the proclivity inside of us which lead us to disobey God and do our own thing. Samson was able to conquer many Philistine enemies but was unable to deal with the burning desire for heathen Philistine women. He burned the Philistines' fields to avenge his wife but was unable or unwilling to allow the Spirit of the LORD to quench the flames of lust raging in his soul.

Both Samson and Samuel were products of praying mothers who had barren wombs. Both mothers vowed no razor would touch their sons head. The difference between Samuel and Samson is that Samuel spent his time in the temple being groomed as a priest of the LORD, while Samson spent a great deal of his time trying to get with heathen women. When you contrast their lives, it is easy to see why Samuel was a mighty man of God, why every word he spoke came to pass, while Samson died amongst the Philistines.

Samson battled with the Philistines for twenty years and died with them but Samuel was able to defeat them with one prayer. When the children of Israel asked Samuel to cry unto the LORD for them for deliverance from the hand of the Philistines, the Bible declares that Samuel offered a sucking lamb as a burnt offering wholly unto the LORD. He did not keep back the best portion for himself as did Hophni and Phinehas the sons of the priest Eli. We have to offer ourselves wholly to God as a burnt offering, a living sacrifice. We have to allow Him to burn out every piece of sin out of our lives. We must give him those areas that we keep hidden because if left unchecked they will fester and grow. When Samuel cried unto the LORD for Israel the LORD heard him.

The LORD thundered with a great thunder and smote them before Israel. Samuel and David had consistent prayer lives and received length of days in the earth and victory over their enemies while Samson and Saul met untimely deaths. Like Samson Saul's ending was not befitting that of a man of God. In his final battle against the Philistines many of the Israelite soldiers fled and were slain. The Philistines followed hard after Saul and his sons. When we are walking in disobedience the devil will try to take out our entire family. They slew Saul's three sons and wounded Saul. As he lay in the field wounded, Saul asked his armourbearer to thrust him through with the sword, but he would not. So *"Saul took a sword, and fell upon it" (1 Samuel 31:4).* The Philistines cut off his head, stripped off his armour, and published his defeat all around their lands and in the house of their idols. They put his armour in the house of Ashtaroth and fastened his body to the wall of Beth-shan, which means house of ease. We will find ease in the house of God where we will live in eternity not in Beth-shan the place of idols. What is the purpose of being in the house of ease if we are dead? We must live in the presence of the LORD not die with the Philistines. Jeremiah said it best when he prophesied the word of the LORD, *"For I know the thoughts that I think toward you, saith the LORD, thoughts of peace, and not of evil, to give you an expected end" (Jeremiah 29:11).* Do not allow the midnight situations to cause you to step out of the will of God. He has an expected end for you in Christ Jesus so you must endure because the night is passing and the light is beginning to shine.

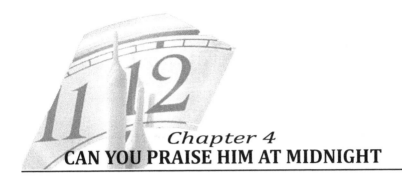

Chapter 4
CAN YOU PRAISE HIM AT MIDNIGHT

We all have to face dark situations at some point in our lives and our posture and our attitude in the night will determine our altitude or lack thereof in the day. My question to you is this; can you praise Him when it appears that darkness is all around you? Praise and worship during the dark seasons of our lives are the evidence that our trust is in God. Murmuring and complaining is evidence there is a lack of trust. It is extremely difficult to see clearly in the midnight hour and that is why we have to trust God to order our steps. *"He will keep the feet of his saints, and the wicked shall be silent in darkness; for by strength shall no man prevail" (1 Samuel 2:9).*

Our praise and worship will confound and confuse the enemies who attack in the midnight hour. The Lord will silence the mouths of those who are speaking evil against us and those who use their tongues to speak words of death over us. He will use our praise in the midnight to accomplish the victory. If you are dealing with a midnight situation at the present time, if your feet are stumbling because wicked people have attacked you, please repeat this scripture right now, *"No weapon that is formed against me shall prosper; and every tongue that shall rise against me in judgment I shall condemn. This is my heritage because I am a servant of the LORD, and my righteousness is of the Lord Jesus."* Your attackers and accusers may appear to be stronger than you but you must believe they will not prevail against you. The plots, schemes and the strategies they have formed against you will not prosper in Jesus' name. Stand still and see the salvation of the Lord your God.

The Lord will keep our feet planted firmly on the solid rock. Feet speak of our walk with Jesus; the Lord will keep the feet of the saint who does not try to handle the midnight situation in his own strength. We cannot fight in the dark so we must understand that Praise is our key to victory. The darker the situation the more we should intensify our praise and our worship.

The scriptures are replete with examples of individuals who praised God radically in the difficulty of their night season. One individual who readily comes to mind is blind Bartimaeus. He sat by a highway begging as Jesus and His disciples came out of Jericho. Jericho was a prosperous town with a good climate. There are many people living in poverty amidst prosperity. Bartimaeus probably received some decent hand outs there but none of it compared with the restoration of his sight. The word Jericho means *"place of fragrance."* Bartimaeus was sitting on the outskirts of the place of fragrance, but there was hope for him, because Jesus left the greatest place of fragrance, heaven. He passed by the place where a blind beggar like Bartimaeus was dealing with a perpetual night life. He was blind, so his world was dark all the time. When he heard that Jesus Christ of Nazareth was passing by he began to cry out. Beloved, sinners need to hear that Jesus is still passing by; they need to know that He can heal all their diseases. We do not need to be silent when it is time to offer up praise and worship unto the LORD. There is a time for quiet meditation but there is also a time to cry out to the LORD our God. It is important to note that when Paul and Silas prayed and sang praises unto God the prisoners heard them. There are prisoners who are bound and they need to hear us praying and singing praises unto the Almighty God. Bartimaeus was imprisoned by his condition of blindness but his hearing was not impaired. God will not allow anyone to be at the point of total debilitation where it is impossible for them to learn of Him. Remember, "Faith comes by hearing and hearing by the word of God." Thank God for the old wives tales, thank God for the nuggets of wisdom I received from my parents and grandparents. All these things have their place but in the midnight hour we will need a word from the Lord.

Jesus is the word that became flesh and we have His word on the inside of us to help us face difficult situations. The word of God will strengthen your faith but the word of doubt will cause you to waver. There are people who criticize radical praise and worship but the preponderance of scripture sets precedent for radical praise and radical worship. When David said, *"I will bless the Lord at all times and His praise shall continually be in my mouth."* He uses the word *tehillah* praise (pronounced the-hil-law); it means laudation a hymn or praise. It comes from the word *halal* (pronounced haw-lal) and it means to shine, to boast, to make a show, to be clamorously foolish, to stultify. Praise in the midnight hour will cause the light to shine. David is saying that is the way God should be praised, unfortunately if you praise God like that in a lot of churches they will ask the deacons to put you out. They want to maintain control of the atmosphere so their man made programs can go forth. They are afraid of losing control. Radical praise and worshipers know that when we let loose and let God our environment will be transformed. Religious folks always attempt to stifle radical praise and worship because they cannot comprehend it. People normally attack and criticize the things they cannot comprehend.

Blind Bartimaeus realized that the Light of the world was passing by and this was his opportunity to escape the dark prison of blindness; he was not going to allow the religious folks to bind him. He cried, *"Jesus, thou son of David, have mercy on me"* (Mark 10:47b). God's mercy will help you out of your midnight situation but you must not allow pride, timidity or any other thing to hinder you from crying out to Him for mercy. Many in the crowd told him to hold his peace but I love the way he responded. Please do not allow the crowd to intimidate you and shut you up when you are praising King Jesus.

The flesh does not want to praise Him and that it is why it has to die daily. We need to take a page out of the book of blind Bartimaeus. When they tried to shut him up he cried louder. We need to follow suit and cry louder when religious devils try to block our praises. Bartimaeus cried, *"Thou son of David, have mercy on me."* The fact that he called Jesus "Son of David" probably irritated some of the people because of its messianic implications. Despite his blindness Bartimaeus was confessing that Jesus was Israel's Messiah. The blind beggar could see who Jesus was and the religious people that should have received light through the law of God were blinded by legalism.

It is a shame when a blind beggar can see more clearly than people who purport to have the eyes of their understanding enlightened. I cannot imagine why people sit in dead churches. This sounds like an oxymoron, but where there is no praise and worship there is not Spirit and where there is no Spirit there is no life. You cannot afford to stay in a dry and barren land because your momma, grand mamma, and your great grand mamma all attended the church. You have to find a place where the Lord is worshipped in the beauty of Holiness. There is a remnant out there that recognizes their need for radical praise and worship. They are the ones who are panting for the presence of the Lord like the deer that pants for the water brook. They know praise and worship opens the flood gates and causes the rain to come down. They will not be silenced. Like Bartimaeus, they will cry louder when the religious crowd attempts to silence them.

God has the mercy we need and we must be radical in our pursuit of it. There is no situation that is so dark that the mercy of God cannot penetrate it. When the Lord heard the cry of the blind beggar, Bartimaeus, He stood still. Our Lord is merciful and in the same manner that a mother will stop in her tracks when she hears the desperate cry of her baby so our Lord will stop and help our infirmities when we cry out to Him. Jesus not only stopped, He commanded Bartimaeus to be brought to Him. We need to get the revelation of the commanded blessing. Earlier we looked at Psalm 42 when the psalmist declared, "Yet the LORD will command his loving-kindness in the daytime." In Psalm 133 a song of degrees that was sung when the Israelites went to the temple, David talks about the place where God commanded the blessing even life forever more. The LORD told Elijah to, "Arise, get thee to Zarephath, which belongeth to Zidon, and dwell there: behold, I have commanded a widow woman there to sustain thee" (1 Kings 17:9). When we look to the Lord as our source he will give us uncommon favor and sustenance through unique and unusual means. When Elijah was at the Brook Cherith he was fed by ravens, birds that are known for neglecting their young; now the LORD's instructions were to go and dwell in enemy territory and be sustained by a widow who was down to a last meal for her and her son. Man's extremities give God opportunity. Elijah was a worshipper, David was a worshipper, the author of psalm 42 was a worshipper and blind Bartimaeus was a worshipper and that is why each received the commanded blessing.

When Jesus commands something it has to be done. Remember, it was Jesus who commanded the winds and the waves to be still when His disciples cowered in the boat. He commanded the devils called legion to come out of the man who was bound with chains and fetters. (Luke 8:29). When Jesus called Bartimaeus the crowd told him to be of good comfort and rise. Imagine if he had allowed the crowd to intimidate him when he cried unto Jesus for mercy. He kept shouting until his breakthrough came. This is the reason why we cannot afford to have our praise silenced by the religious crowd. Keep shouting until the breakthrough comes. When the Lord hears our midnight praise He will comfort us and cause us to rise from the darkness of our situation. When the prodigal son came to himself he said, "I will arise and go to my father" (Luke 15:18). We cannot fall so far away from our Father's House where a prayer of repentance cannot lead us home. We must will ourselves to arise. He was in the pig pen desiring to eat the husk which the pigs ate, but he remembered that in his father's house the servants had bread enough to spare. When Bartimaeus heard that Jesus called for him, he arose.

Bartimaeus cast off his garment and went to Jesus. Cloaks were used as a coat during cold weather and as bedding at night. Bartimaeus may have spread it before him when be begged. Casting it off meant he realized by faith that Jesus was calling him into a new life and he would not need a beggar's garment anymore. Jesus healed his eyes and told him that his faith had made him whole. Faith without works is dead and blind Bartimaeus received light in his eyes because he believed in Jesus as Messiah and acted in faith by crying out until Jesus granted his request. Praise in the midnight hour is an exercise in faith. It is evidence that we believe God although we are unable to see deliverance. Are you at the midnight hour of a dark situation right now? Take a moment to cry out to Jesus, because He is full of mercy and He will hear and answer your cry.

JAIL HOUSE ROCK

One of my favorite verses in the Bible is Acts 16:25 because it tells the encouraging story of Paul and Silas's posture of prayer and praise in an inner prison at midnight. It is one thing to be in prison but it is something entirely different when you are in an inner prison. Serving a prison sentence is tough enough with the loss of your freedom and the separation from loved ones. When you have to spend time in segregation it makes the sentence tougher. The Apostle Paul and his fellow minister Silas were beaten and thrown into a prison because they had cast a familiar spirit out of a young girl that brought her masters much gain through fortune telling. The devil was mad because God opened the heart of Lydia to receive the gospel and she in turn opened her house to Paul and his companions to have church meetings there. The jailer decided to fasten their feet in stocks and place them in an inner prison to ensure they would not escape. It is bad enough to be beaten but your problems are compounded when your feet are fastened with stocks and you are thrown into an inner prison. What the jailer did not understand was that they were not going to attempt a break out because God was going to break in. Hallelujah!!! A Roman jailer would have to forfeit his life if he lost a prisoner so the jailer wanted to make sure they were secured. There are times when our problems are compounded in the midnight hour but our posture of praise must remain. There are many people that adopt a posture of murmuring, complaining and the handing out of blame when a calamity strikes. I believe we can learn a great deal from the people in the Bible that survived their midnight experiences. The jailer went to sleep because he felt the prisoners were secured. He did not understand the fact that praise in the midnight can cause a breach in the inner prison. Here is the crux or the conclusion to the matter, here is the antidote for the enemy's bite at midnight, here is the key to your deliverance. *"And at midnight Paul and Silas prayed, and sang praises unto God: and the prisoners heard them"* (Acts 16:25). The Greek word for praises in Acts 16:25 is *humneo* and it means to "celebrate (God) in song: sing a hymn (praise unto)." There are some key revelation nuggets to be gleaned from this verse.

The men of God did not murmur or complain they just prayed and sang praises unto God. Midnight is not an easy time to sing the song of the Lord but if you can sing at midnight you can expect to receive deliverance from the Lord. "Any fool can sing in the day, "said Charles Haddon Spurgeon. "It is easy to sing when we can read the notes by daylight but the sum singer is he who can sing when there is not a ray of light to read by... Songs in the night come only from God; they are not in the power of men." Acts 16:26 declares, *"And suddenly there was a great earthquake, so that the foundations of the prison were shaken: and immediately all the doors were opened, and every one's bands were loosed."* That is what a midnight halal praise will do.

It is one thing to experience an earthquake but it is entirely another thing to experience a great earthquake. When you give Him the halal praise at midnight He knows that you mean business. Anyone can praise God while it is light and things are going well. Can you give Him a midnight bright shining clamorously foolish stultifying praise? When the man you planned on marrying decides you are not the one? Can you halal Him when your husband of many years decides to leave because he wants a younger woman? Can you halal him when you have been betrayed by someone you trusted? When you have contracted a sexually transmitted disease from someone you thought was committed to you, can you halal Him? Can you halal Him when that disease is incurable according to the doctor's prognosis? What ever your midnight situation just give Jesus a radical praise and tell Him for God you live.

My God, if a bunch of prisoners can give Him such a radical praise at midnight that caused a great earthquake and a shaking of the foundations of the prison then surely you can praise Him in the midnight of your situation. Remember, the word foundations is plural meaning every part of the very things that held the prison was shaken.

I believe Psalm 18 gives us a picture of how God manifested in the prison at midnight as Paul and Silas prayed and sang praise. David declared, *The LORD is my rock, and my fortress, and my deliverer; my God, my strength, in whom I will trust; my buckler, and the horn of my salvation, and my high tower. I will call upon the LORD, who is worthy to be praised: so shall I be saved from mine enemies. The sorrows of death compassed me, and the floods of ungodly men made me afraid. The sorrows of hell compassed me about: the snares of death prevented me. In my distress I called upon the LORD, and cried unto my God: he heard my voice out of his temple, and my cry came before him, even into his ears. Then the earth shook and trembled; the foundations also of the hills moved and were shaken, because he was wroth.*

There went up a smoke out of his nostrils, and fire out of his mouth devoured: coals were kindled by it. He bowed the heavens also, and came down: and darkness was under his feet. And he rode upon a cherub, and did fly: yea, he did fly upon the wings of the wind. He made darkness his secret place; his pavilion round about him were dark waters and thick clouds of the skies. At the brightness that was before him his thick clouds passed, hail stones and coals of fire. The LORD also thundered in the heavens, and the Highest gave his voice; hail stones and coals of fire. Yea, he sent out his arrows, and scattered them; and he shot out lightnings, and discomfited them. Then the channels of waters were seen, and the foundations of the world were discovered at thy rebuke, O LORD, at the blast of the breath of thy nostrils. It is important to note, when David said God is worthy to be praised he used the word halal. He said he was surrounded by the sorrows of death and ungodly men came against him like a flood. David was compassed by death and hell. In his distress he called upon the Lord and cried unto God and God heard him from his temple and shook the foundations of the earth and caused them to tremble; the hills moved and were shaken.

It is not easy to praise God when everything around you appears to be falling apart but if you can muster enough strength to praise Him at midnight you can get a sudden breakthrough. Can you see the pattern? He shook foundations for David, He shook them for Paul and Silas, and he will shake them for you and me. They cried unto the LORD and He heard them and He will hear our cry because He is not a respecter of persons. It may appear as if He is taking a long time to come, but let me tell you this, when He shows up He shows up in a big way. Is it not awesome to know that darkness was under His feet? The revelation there is He walks on the things that cause us distress. Jesus walked on the water that was boisterous during the storm the disciples encountered on their way to the other side and He will walk on the troubles when we cry out to Him.

I love the fact that the manifest presence of God in the inner prison meant an immediate opening of the prison doors and the loosing of every prisoner's bands. I believe we can experience this type of manifestation today if we are willing to come beyond the borders of religion and give Him a halal praise. The beauty of the visitation was not only that Paul and Silas' prison door and bands were loosed but also that of all the other prisoners. That is correct; there was not one prisoner that was left in chains. This is the reason why your midnight praise is so important. It is not for your deliverance alone but God will use it to open the prison doors for others.

When the keeper of the prison woke up he drew his sword because he thought all the prisoners had fled. How he was able to sleep through the Jail House Rock, the earthquake and the shaking of the foundations, I know, God must have made a deep sleep come upon him so he would not be able to interfere with the midnight praise celebration. When he finally awoke He was going to kill himself because he thought he had lost all the prisoners. Paul had to yell out to him not to take his own life because no one had left the prison. Can you imagine that? The prisoners' doors were open, the bands were loosed but none of the prisoners wanted to escape, do you want to know why? The Spirit of the Lord was in the prison and where the Spirit of the Lord is there is liberty. When the Lord is in the prison the prison is worth being in. The prisoners did not break out because the Almighty God had broken in. I know there were many times during my incarceration on the Isle of Sheppy in England when the Spirit of the Lord was in the Bible study, and no one wanted to leave to go back to their own cell. I remember one particular instance when one of the prisoners was giving his heart to the Lord and a guard came to the door and told us it was time for everyone to get back to their own cells. I shut the cell door and said it is more important to obey God. A friend that was there told me several years later that he thought for sure we were all going to the block that night. The block is also called solitary confinement and that is where an inmate is taken for breaking prison rules. The guard waited until we were finished before he came back.

When Paul spoke to the keeper of the prison assuring him that all prisoners were present; He came trembling and fell down before them. Our midnight praise will make our enemies tremble. Is that not amazing? The prisoner was trembling before Paul and Silas because he saw the evidence of the midnight praise. He spoke to Paul and Silas and said, "Sirs, what must I do to be saved." An individual whose only concern was putting the men of God in the inner prison is now seeking the key to salvation. Your greatest testimony to people will come out of your ability to praise God in the midnight hour. We have to understand that praise is one of the most potent weapons in the believer's arsenal. Praise ascribes honor and Glory to our God but it also routs the enemy and opens the brass heaven so the blessings of God can flow to us. I believe this is one of the reasons the enemy fights us so hard when it is time to praise the Lord. He knows when we are bold enough to praise the name of our God in the midst of our trials it sends confusion into his camp.

The Psalmist wrote, *"My tears have been my meat day and night, while they continually say unto me, where is thy God? When I remember these things, I pour out my soul in me: for I had gone with the multitude, I went with them to the house of God, with the voice of joy and praise, with a multitude that kept holy day. Why art thou cast down, O my soul? And why art thou disquieted in me? Hope thou in God: for I shall yet praise him for the help of his countenance. O my God, my soul is cast down within me: therefore will I remember thee from the land of Jordan, and of the Hermonites, from the hill Mizar. Deep calleth unto deep at the noise of thy waterspouts: all thy waves and thy billows are gone over me. Yet the Lord will command his loving-kindness in the daytime, and in the night his song shall be with me, and my prayer unto the God of my life" (Psalm 42:3-8).*

God gives us songs in the night and it is those songs that help us to make it to the new day so we can see and experience his loving kindness. There are certain things we have to face in the midnight hour that the multitude cannot help us with. When sorrows are compassing us day and night there is a serious need for some songs in the night. When we face those situations only God can intervene on our behalf. You know you are dealing with a midnight situation when your tears are flowing day and night. The Hebrew word for meat is lechem and it means food, especially bread, or grain. It comes from the word lacham which means to feed on, to consume, to battle. You are in a dire strait when your tears are your bread. There was a time when the Psalmist went with the multitude with the voice of joy and praise to the house of God. Something happened that caused the soul of the psalmist to be cast down. He was in a deep state of depression and felt overwhelmed by his enemies; he compared their attacks to a storm coming over him like great billows. It was as if he was being hit by a flood, one wave after another. There are times when the enemy will come against us like a flood but we must remember God's promise to lift up a standard against Him. I believe that standard is prayer and halal praise. His prayer was synonymous with his praise. His tears were his meat day and night but he was confident that the LORD would command his loving kindness in the daytime and his praise would be from a song in the night.

Anyone who has had to deal with deep depression and a melancholy mood knows how lonely and dark those places are. You feel as if you are being overwhelmed and there is no one to help. If you flow in the prophetic anointing that is one of the spirits you will have to deal with. Elijah was depressed and living in a cave because he felt that all the people had forsaken God for the prophets of Baal and he was the only left standing for God. Never allow yourself to feel alone and isolated in the midnight season, know that you are part of a remnant. Find someone of like precious faith and get that individual to pray with you. Draw from the well that is deep within you and offer up prayer and praise unto the Almighty God. The hope of the psalmist was in God and he knew he had to praise Him. Although his soul was disquieted and cast down he would not quit; he said "I will yet praise Him for the help of His countenance." The Hebrew word for praise here is *yadah* and it means to hold out or extend the hands, to revere or worship (with extended hands). When we extend our hands in reverence and worship unto the Lord he will fill them with blessings.

I believe Paul and Silas were familiar with this Psalm and the principle of praying and singing the song of the Lord at night. There is something marvelous and wonderful about giving God a radical praise in the midnight hour. I believe when the prisoners heard Paul and Silas praying and praising God, a praise celebration broke out. When that happened, there was a shaking in the prison. In Psalm 22:3 David declared, *"But thou art holy, O thou that inhabitest the praises of*

Israel." The Hebrew word for inhabitest is yashab and it means to sit down (specifically as judge. In ambush, in quiet); to dwell, to remain, to settle or to marry." What an awesome revelation. God sits or settles in the praise of His people waiting to ambush their enemies. There is a great need for in-depth teaching on the importance of praise and worship. Later on, we will see how God set ambushes up against the enemies of Judah when Jehoshaphat and the people sang and praised God for the beauty of His Holiness and His enduring mercies. David used the same Hebrew word for praises in Psalm 22 that he used in Psalm 34 when he declared, *"His praise shall continue to be in my mouth."* Remember it is the word *tehillah* and it means laudation, a hymn of praise. It comes from the word halal which means to shine, to make a show, to boast, to rave, to celebrate. I would say that is the type of praise Paul and Silas gave at midnight. They had a celebration in the prison that energized the other prisoners. Paul and Silas were the sons of God and when the sons of God praise Him He is going to manifest. He will manifest because He inhabits their praise waiting to set ambushes against their enemy. When God manifests, there will be a quaking, a shaking, and a shift that causes darkness to give way to His marvelous light.

SEND JUDAH FIRST

Although midnight is not the time we feel like praying and singing praises unto God it has to be the time we make a conscious effort to do so. Our flesh does not want to praise God so when we are struggling with a dark situation the flesh would love nothing more than to impose its will. Someone said, "When the enemy starts messing God will start blessing." I believe that blessing comes when we are able to press past the obstacles and give God praise. When we praise, God will give us a raise. When the Lord established the arrangement of the Israelite camp for their journey into Canaan the moving procession was led by the tribe of Judah and Judah means praise. "Now after the death of Joshua it came to pass, that the children of Israel asked the LORD saying, "Who shall go up for us against the Canaanites first, to fight against them? And the LORD said, Judah shall go up: behold, I have delivered the land into his hand" (Judges 1:1-2). Judah should always go up first. The praise has to go up because when the praise goes up, the blessings of deliverance come down.

Our first response to any midnight situation should be prayer and praise, and it would be helpful to do some fasting also.

One of the best examples of sending Judah first is found in the book of Chronicles. Jehoshaphat and the kingdom of Judah had come under attack from a three nation confederation of Amon, Moab, and Mount Sier. King Jehoshaphat was told that a great multitude had come against Judah and his response was to seek the Lord and to proclaim a fast throughout all Judah. The King and his people faced a midnight situation when they were surrounded by enemies. They used the weapon of prayer and praise to defeat their enemies. When the King and the people stood before the Lord the Bible says, "Then upon Jahaziel the son of Zechariah, the son of Benaiah, the son of Jeiel, the son of Mattaniah, a Levite of the sons of Asaph, came the Spirit of the Lord in the midst of the congregation" (2 Chronicles 20:14). The Spirit of the Lord did not come up on anyone; He came upon a descendant of Asaph. He was a Levite and one of the leaders of David's choir. He is mentioned along with King David as being skilled in music and, as a "seer." Jahaziel is one of his descendants and that is why it is no accident or coincidence that the word of the Lord came to him for the people of Judah. People who love to praise and worship God will experience a prophetic word that will come from the manifestation of the Spirit of the Lord. Jahaziel told the king and the people not to be afraid because the battle was not theirs but the Lords. This is the reason why we send Judah first. When midnight comes and we are having a praise party, the demons will be confused because they will not be able to figure out how we can maintain our praise in the midst of a dark situation. Your praise says I cannot win this battle on my own so I am trusting God to fight if for me. God loves when we put our trust in Him. Through Jahaziel the Lord instructed them where to go to find the enemy. I love the instructions the Lord gave King Jehoshaphat. "Ye shall not need to fight this battle: set yourselves, stand ye still, and see the salvation of the LORD with you, O Judah and Jerusalem: fear not, nor be dismayed; tomorrow go out against them for the LORD will be with you. And Jehoshaphat bowed his head with his face to the ground: and all Judah and the inhabitants of Jerusalem fell before the LORD, worshipping the LORD. And the Levites, of the children of the Kohathites, and of the children of the Korhites, stood up to praise the LORD God of Israel with a loud voice on high" (2 Chronicles 20:17-18). Remember at midnight Paul and Silas prayed and sang unto the Lord loud enough so the prisoners heard them. Remember Bartimaeus refused to allow the religious folks to silence his cry when he needed deliverance from his blindness. Now, here are the people of Judah praising God with a loud voice on high. So much for the people who say, "it does not take all that" when they hear us praising God with a loud voice on high. Our response should be, "If you had my testimony, you would have my praise." If you only knew what the Lord has brought me through, then you would understand the level of my praise. The darker my midnight the louder my praise; we have to stop worrying about offending people and learn to give God praise. In his beautiful Hymn Charles Jones wrote, "I will make the darkness light before thee, what is wrong I'll make it right before thee, all thy battles I will fight before thee, and the high place I'll bring down." Praise makes dark places illuminate with light; praise breaks yokes and makes burdens light.

Instead of appointing archers and soldiers with other weapons, Jehoshaphat appointed singers unto the LORD that praised the beauty of His holiness. That seems like a strange battle strategy for a people surrounded by hostile enemies but they understood that praise was their most potent weapon. And when they began to sing and praise, the LORD set ambushes against the children of Ammon, Moab, and mount Seir and smote them. Praise in the midst of our fiercest battles will snatch victory from the jaws of defeat. The enemies of Judah turned on one another and destroyed each other. None of the enemy escaped, remember when Paul and Silas prayed and praised all the prison doors were opened and every prisoner's bands were loosed. It is no different with you and me if we are willing to praise him in the midst of our adversity. "And when Jehoshaphat and his people came to take away the spoil of them, they found among them in abundance both riches with the dead bodies, and precious jewels, which they stripped off for themselves, more than they could carry away: and they were three days in gathering of the spoil, it was so much" (2

Chronicles 20:25). Your midnight praise will not only defeat your enemies it will take you into overflow. It will cause you to receive a prophetic word that will tell you the location of the enemy and the strategy to defeat him. And on the fourth day they assembled themselves in the valley of Berachah; for there they blessed the LORD: therefore the name of the same place was called, The valley of Berachah, unto this day. The word Berachah means blessing. They were three days in gathering the spoils and on the fourth day they assembled themselves in a place called blessing. Then they returned, every man of Judah and Jerusalem, and Jehoshaphat in the forefront of them, to go again to Jerusalem with joy; for the LORD had made them to rejoice over their enemies. And they came to Jerusalem with psalteries and harps and trumpets unto the house of the LORD" (2 Chronicles 20:26-28).

The blessings were reciprocal. They received blessings from the LORD, and they blessed the LORD. Jehoshaphat was in the forefront leading the praises. I am perplexed when I go to a church and the pastor and other leaders sit stoically during worship while the congregation is actively praising and worshiping the Lord. As soon as they get the microphone, many of them will start exhorting and pumping the people to praise the Lord. Sometimes I want to jump up and ask them what they thought we were doing all the time they sat stoically. I cannot stress enough the importance of our praise and worship. One of the things you will notice in the Bible about people who came to Jesus seeking healing for their loved ones is their willingness to fall down and worship him. *"And, behold there came a leper and worshipped Him, saying, Lord, if thou wilt, thou canst make me clean" (Matthew 8:2).*

SOLDIERS, IN THE ARMY OF THE LORD

Gideon's story is a great example of the child of God's ability to gain victory when the odds are against him and the attack is coming from all sides. During the period of the Judges the people were in constant rebellion against God. Before his death, Joshua gathered the people and reminded them of the deliverance they had received from the hand of the Lord. The people promised not to forsake the Lord and serve other gods. Once the generation died that agreed not to forsake the Lord, the next generation did evil in the sight of the Lord. The Lord raised up judges to rule the people and lead them into battle when they cried unto him for protection from their enemies. Gideon was one of the judges raised up by the Lord.

The children of Israel's rebellion caused them to fall under the domination of the Midianites. *"And so it was, when Israel had sown, that the Midianites came up, and the Amalekites, and the children of the east, even they came up against them; And they encamped against them, and destroyed the increase of the earth, till thou come unto Gaza, and left no sustenance for Israel, neither sheep, nor ox, nor ass" (Judges 6:3-4).* The plan of the enemy is to destroy us by wiping out all of our substance. Gideon was threshing out wheat by the winepress in-order to hide it from the enemy. While threshing he received a visitation from the angel of the Lord. When the enemy has launched an all out attack against us, we should expect angelic visitation. God will not leave us alone to face the attacks that are coming against us. We must have an expectation that when the enemy comes in like a flood the Spirit of the LORD will lift up a standard against him. Although Gideon is hiding and cowering like the rest of the Israelites the angel says something very interesting to him. "The Lord is with thee, thou mighty man of valor." The Hebrew word for valor is chayil (pronounced khah-yil); it means an army, wealth, virtue, power, and riches. At that point in his life Gideon looked like anything but a mighty man of valor. He did not have an army and he certainly did not have power and riches. We have to remember that God does not see us only where we are at the present time; He has the panoramic view in that He sees everything all at once, He sees the ending from the beginning. God is the one who can command light to shine out of darkness; He can bring life out of death, and create something out of nothing. In many instances we speak the problem instead of the solution.

The angel knew the condition of Gideon and the nation so it made no sense to remind him of the things that had befallen them; he spoke to Gideon in reference to where the LORD was taking him not where he was. In his letter to the church at Rome the Apostle Paul addressed the issue of justification of faith by explaining how God took an elderly man whose wife was barren and past child bearing years and gave them a child. Paul declared "even God, who quickeneth the dead, and calleth those things which be not as though they are" (Romans 4:17). We have a tendency to spend an inordinate amount of time focusing on our problems, and on our shortcomings but God sees beyond our limitations; He sees us as victorious in Jesus Christ. Believe the report of the LORD in every trial you face.

We do not deny the reality of any situation but we have confidence that the LORD of Hosts will make us the victors and not the vanquished. He will make us the head and not the tail, above and not beneath. We have to believe it for ourselves. If you feel pressed by the enemy at the present time, if you feel as if you are being bombarded on every side, speak those things that are not as though they already are. If you are suffering from an infirmity, sickness or disease, look in your Bible and quote the scriptures where God has promised to heal His people. If you are devastated because you have been abandoned by a spouse, a child or someone else that you love, please be reminded that Jesus will never leave you or forsake you. He is an ever present help in the time of trouble. Do not faint or become weary because your due season is coming and you will reap.

Gideon could not understand why so many calamities had befallen the people if God was with them. This is one of the great mysteries. Many people cannot understand why they get afflicted with some incurable disease when they are serving God to the best of their ability. God does not put sickness on His children but He will use it for His Glory, so we have to trust Him. Gideon wanted to know where all the miracles were that were spoken to them by their fathers. There are many people who want to see a miracle before they believe God but faith dictates that I believe Him even if I do not witness a miracle. It is easy to second guess and question God when we are waiting on the fulfillment of His promise. It is the trials and the tribulations that prepare us to handle the fulfilled promises without taking the glory for ourselves.

Gideon suffered from unbelief and low self esteem. The angel told him that he was chosen to deliver Israel but the whole idea seemed ludicrous to him. He told the angel, "Behold my family is poor in Manasseh, and I am the least in my father's house." When God gets ready to use us He does not care if our family was on food stamps, wick, and government cheese. He does not care if we are the least in our family because we went to prison, did not graduate from college, or we are working a menial job for minimum wage. God loves to take alley cats and transform them into aristocrats. Saul had a similar response of stage fright when Samuel told him that all the desire of Israel was on him and on all his father's house. Saul declared, "Am not I a Benjamite, of the smallest of the tribes of Israel? And my family the least of all the families of the tribe of Benjamin? Wherefore then speakest thou so to me? (1 Samuel 9:21). God loves to take little things and accomplish great things with them. He took a babe born in a manger and made Him the Christ, the King; the Prophet Micah spoke about it when he declared, *"But thou, Bethlehem Ephratah, though thou be little among the thousands of Judah, yet out of thee shall he come forth unto me that is to be ruler in Israel; whose goings forth have been from of old, everlasting" (Micha 5:2).* Out of Judah, out of the place of praise God will bring forth things in your life that will give you the authority to overcome and remain. Your life might appear as if it is not going anywhere fast but God sees a diamond in the rough. You only see a piece of coal, but He sees the diamond polished and glistening. You see the dross but He sees the gold refined, polished, and sitting on display in the window of the kingdom jewelry store. Do not focus on the darkness of the situation, Do not focus on the dross , Do not focus on the fact that your credit is tore up from the floor up, or the fact that your bank account is empty and your checks are bouncing like a Spalding basketball. You may have more bills than Clinton, but stand on the promises of God and allow Him to finish the work He has started.

The angel continued to reassure Gideon that he was chosen by God to deliver the Israelites from the domination of the Midianites. Gideon was so full of doubt that the angel had to show him some signs for him to believe. It is better to trust than to doubt but God's plan for our lives will be fulfilled even if He has to show us some signs to make us believe. *"Then Jerubbaal, who is Gideon, and all the people that were with him, rose up early, and pitched beside the well of Harod: so that the host of the Midianites were of the north side of them, by the hill of Moreh, in the valley" (Judges 7:1).* It appears that Gideon gathered as many people as he could because he felt there is strength in numbers. In the natural realm that axiom may be true, but God can deliver with many and He can deliver with few. If Gideon was able to defeat the enemy with a great army then the army would get all the credit. *"And the LORD said unto Gideon, The people that are with thee are too many for me to give the Midianites into their hands, lest Israel vaunt themselves against me, saying, Mine own hand hath save me" (Judges 7:2).* The flesh is always trying to glorify itself and God will have none of that. There are valuable lessons to be learned in the scriptures on why we must put our trust in the LORD our God and not in the strength of our possessions. When David numbered Israel God sent a pestilence upon Israel that killed seventy thousand men. God will not allow us to be puffed up with pride because we think we have won the battle with our own strength and ingenuity. There are times He will strip us of certain possessions prior to us going into battle so we will rely completely on him. God allowed me to be laid off from the company I worked for because He was preparing me to travel and preach the gospel. He wanted me to trust Him for my provision. In conjunction with the layoff He dried up the cleaning business that my wife and her cousin had, and allowed some of my wife's personal clients to release her. The 401k that I amassed was spent quicker than I was able to save it. When the company called me back to work I could sense the Lord saying, *"If you go back you will have the leaks and the onions but if you keep looking ahead to the work I have called you to do I will bless you."*

I must admit that for a split second I thought about the paychecks and the matching 401k but I had far too many testimonies of God's deliverance in the midnight hour not to trust it at that crucial moment. When I told the HR person on the phone that I was going in another direction it meant my unemployment dried up. Unemployment might not supply everything you need but it is better than nothing. It is not very difficult to trust and have faith after losing a job when you have other resources like a cleaning business and unemployment, but it is very challenging when those resources begin to dry up. Drought and famine will separate the faith talkers from the faith walkers. Many people talk a good game but lose heart when it is time to put their money where their mouth is. It is time to put up or shut up. If we say we believe God then we should not be having heart palpitations when the midnight hour comes upon us. We are in a season where many saints are losing jobs, their houses are being foreclosed, they are being evicted from apartments, and their cars are being repossessed. The brooks which formerly sustained them have dried up and many of them are discombobulated, stressed, depressed, and oppressed. All the prosperity messages they have heard in the past have not borne much fruit and many of them do not know what to do. My advice to you if you are in that situation is to keep trusting God, keep praying and keep on praising.

God will dry up some resources in-order to move us from one place to another. There are individuals to whom God has given the gift of entrepreneurship but they have become complacent because of the provisions provided by their Job. God desires to take them to a place of overflow but they cannot see how they could survive if they left the job. God will allow the job to be sent overseas to propel them into entrepreneurship. Praise is our expression of trust; it is evidence that we believe God for more than what the natural eye can see. If your Job or business has dried up, if your marriage has dried up, if your unemployment is about to run out, if you are busted, disgusted and can barely be trusted, please do not be discouraged. God is refining you and propelling you to your next dimension in Him. God will not allow you to go into a new place with an old mindset; it is not wise to put new wine into old wine skins.

God was about to cut the number of Gideon's army and He would do it by getting rid of those that were afraid. Fear is crippling and it will cause us to stay in an uncomfortable unproductive place because we like to be around things that are familiar. Abram was counted righteous because he stepped out of the familiar into the unfamiliar because God told him to. If we are going to come to a place of divine destiny and purpose we will have to step out of the familiar and allow God to take us to some new places. God instructed Gideon to proclaim in the ears of the people these words; *"Whosoever is fearful and afraid, let him return and depart early from mount Gilead" (Judges 7:3).* God does not waste time so He decided to get rid of the fearful ones early. It makes no sense to carry people into battle with you who are afraid of their own shadow. In this season you need people who are willing to stand in the face of the opposition of the enemy and wage war in the realm of the spirit. You do not need people who are going to cut and run as soon as the camp takes a hit. We need soldiers who will stand while the enemy is firing his missiles at us from every corner.

22,000 people left after the proclamation, and 10,000 remained. God told Gideon that the 10,000 was still too many. He instructed Gideon to *"bring them down unto the water to be tried."* He told Gideon that the ones who lapped the water with their tongues like a dog should be set aside, and the ones who bowed their knees to drink should also be set aside. There were 300 men who lapped, and God chose the 300 to give deliverance to the nation and sent the rest home. The number 300 represents the faithful remnant. (Genesis 5:22, 6:15, Judges 8:4, 15:4). It does not matter how much darkness envelopes this world, God has a faithful remnant that has not bowed their knees to Baal. These are the hidden ones creation is groaning for. They are the sons of God who are being prepared to deliver the earth from its groaning. Through the furnace of affliction they are being purified to carry God's Glory, His weight, His splendor. They have been living in tabernacles like Abraham, endured years of barreness like Sarai, betrayed by their own family and were thrown in a pit like Joseph. They were lied on in Potiphar's house and forgotten by people they helped in prison. They were in the desert of Midian like Moses, in the cave of Adullam like David, in the fiery furnace like the three Hebrew boys Shadrach, Meshach, and Abed-nego, slapped around and thrown into a cistern like Jeremiah, trusted God in captivity like Ezekiel, survived the lion's den like Daniel, said "if I perish I perish, like Esther," and overcame their wilderness temptation like Jesus. It was time for Gideon to snatch victory from the clutches of defeat like so many of his ancestors before him. He was about to witness firsthand the Power and Might of the God of Israel his fathers spoke about.

He was told a dream detailing the manner in which he and the army would be victorious. He was told that *"a cake of barley bread tumbled into the host of Midian, and came unto a tent, and smote it that it fell, and overturned it, that the tent lay along"* (Judges 7:13-15). When he heard the dream and the interpretation Gideon responded with worship. It gave him the confidence he needed because he finally realized the Lord was with him. In the midnight hour God will visit us in dreams and visions and will give us the blueprint for victory. This is why it is imperative that we find a place in praise and worship once we have prayed. Praise and worship please God and releases the prophetic anointing. Show me someone with a prophetic anointing and I will show you a worshipper; they go hand in hand. The point of praising God in the midnight hour has to be stressed because it is one of the key components to breaking through at midnight. An example of praise and worship and the prophetic is found In 1 Samuel 10. Samuel took a vial of oil and poured it upon Saul's head signifying the LORD had anointed him to be captain over His inheritance. God's inheritance is His people. Samuel gave Saul explicit instructions. In part of the instructions Samuel said, *"After that thou shalt come to the hill of God, where is the garrison of the Philistines: and it shall come to pass, when thou art come thither to the city, that thou shalt meet a company of prophets coming down from the high place with a psaltery, and a tabret, and a pipe, and a harp, before them; and they shall prophecy."* It is interesting that the garrison of the Philistines is at the hill of God. The devil is relentless in his pursuit of the people of God.

Notice the company of prophets were coming down from the high place. True prophets worship God until they break through the garrison of Philistines camped near the hill of God. Once they get to the hill of God, or the high place they received prophetic revelation from, the mouth of God which they bring down to the people. I said true prophets not profits. Notice that the psaltery, the tabret, the pipe and the harp were before them. Praise should always be before us. Samuel told Saul that, *"the Spirit of the LORD will come upon thee, and thou shalt prophesy with them, and shalt be turned into another man."* Praise and worship facilitates and is conducive to the entrance of the Spirit of the LORD upon the worshipper. Praise and worship opens the door for the people of God to prophesy. Please hear me for this is extremely important. Worship will turn you and me into another man because it takes the focus and the attention off of us and places it where it belongs, it belongs on the LORD.

Gideon's battle strategy was to put a trumpet in every man's hand with empty pitchers and lamps in the pitchers. Trumpets represent symbols of gathering, the coming of Christ, judgment, and blessing.

(1 Corinthians 14:8; Exodus 19:13-16; Joshua 6:5; 1 Samuel 13:3; 2 Samuel 2:28). Trumpets were used only by the priests in announcing the approach of festivals and in giving signals of war. We are modern day priests of the Lord Jesus and we have to lift our voices in worship like a trumpet. When we do that we announce the judgment of the LORD and the blessing of the LORD. In the midnight hour we must resist the attempts of the adversary to keep us in a state of pity. We must lift our voices like a trumpet and shout unto God with the voice of triumph. Anyone can shout when the battle is won, but can you shout at midnight? Can you shout when you have three hundred soldiers but you are surrounded by thousands of Midianites? Can you shout when you only have a few dollars but thousands of dollars worth of bills? Can you shout when you have no health insurance but your body is aching with pain and you are facing financial ruin because of unpaid medical bills? Can you shout in the middle of the night when all is dark and you cannot see the light? Do not wait for the battle to be over, shout now. Lift up your voice like a trumpet in Zion because you are one praise away from your breakthrough!

Gideon divided his army of Three hundred into three companies. Gideon took one hundred men with him and went to the outside of the Midianite camp. It was the beginning of the middle watch which was midnight. The enemy thinks we are going to wallow in despair at midnight but he does not realize that we have praise and are about to launch an attack against his camp in the middle of the night. Gideon and his men held the trumpets in their right hand and the pitcher in their left. They blew the trumpets, and broke the pitchers that were in their hands. The pitcher or the vessel has to be broken so the light can come forth. The treasure is in earthen vessels so God gets the glory. When we die to the flesh and allow God to break us the light of the Holy Ghost can shine. The Bible declares, *"And they stood every man in his place round about the camp: and all the host ran, and cried, and fled" (Judges 7:21).* When we stand in our assigned place, allow our light to shine, and blow the trumpet of praise, the enemy will have to flee. At midnight just stay in your lane and allow the LORD to direct the traffic and there will not be an accident.

Midnight is a dark time but it is not the time to cower and be fearful. It is a time that we must be on the offensive. It is not the time to lament, it is the time to pray and praise. When people who are bound see and hear us praying and praising at midnight it will help them receive deliverance.

Chapter 5
THE MIDNIGHT CRY

**"And at midnight there was a cry made, behold, the
bridegroom cometh; go ye out to meet him"**

The book of Exodus tells us of the deliverance of the children of
Israel from bondage in Egypt. Egypt is symbolic of the world's
system that has people bound. Pharaoh the leader of Egypt was
considered a god. The LORD sent 10 plagues upon the nation to
convince them to free the Israelites. The final plague was the death of
the first born. "And Moses said, Thus saith the LORD, About midnight
will I go out into the midst of Egypt: And all the firstborn in the land
of Egypt shall die, from the firstborn of Pharaoh that sitteth upon
his throne, even unto the firstborn of the maidservant that is behind
the mill; and all the firstborn of beasts. And there shall be a great cry
throughout all the land of Egypt, such as there was none like it, nor
shall be like it any more" (Exodus 11:4-6).

There would be no person or beast that would be exempt from
the 10th plague, not even Pharaoh. Ten is the number of law, order,
and restoration. God was about to deliver His people from Egypt in-
order to give them His law and to use them to birth the Messiah so
all things could be restored by the redemption Jesus' death, burial,
and resurrection provided. Redemption has always been the plan of
God since the fall of Adam. *"And every firstling of an ass thou shalt
redeem with a lamb; and if thou wilt not redeem it, then thou shalt
break his neck: and all the firstborn of man among thy children shalt
thou redeem" (Exodus 13:13).* God has to have preeminence in the
earth because the first of everything belongs to Him. Since Pharaoh

was considered a god He did not give the God of heaven glory. God demonstrated his preeminence by striking the firstborn of man and beast in Egypt. This is why giving God the tithe or the tenth is so important. It is important because it demonstrates the fact that He has preeminence in our lives. It is important that we give Him the first tenth not just any tenth.

When God instituted the Passover feast with the killing of a lamb without spot or blemish it was a type of fulfillment by Jesus Christ, the paschal lamb. The Passover was instituted on the tenth day of the month.

The Bible says, *"And it came to pass, that at midnight the LORD smote all the firstborn in the land of Egypt, from the firstborn of Pharaoh that sat on his throne unto the firstborn of the captive that was in the dungeon; and all the firstborn of cattle. And Pharaoh rose up in the night, he, and all his servants, and all the Egyptians; and there was a great cry in Egypt; for there was not a house where there was not one dead" (Exodus 11:29-30).* The Israelites were the only people in Egypt that did not suffer loss that midnight. God's people have nothing to fear at midnight.

DO YOU FEEL FORSAKEN?

The midnight cry for Jesus came as He hung on the cross between two thieves. Two is the number of witness and separation. There was darkness on the land from the sixth hour until the ninth hour. Six is the number of man, beast and Satan. Man was created on the sixth day. There are six generations of Cain. Nine is the number of finality, fullness, fruitfulness, and the number of the fruit of the womb. God the Son came in the likeness of a man to die on the cross to finish the work of salvation so we could walk in the fullness and the fruitfulness of the Holy Ghost. "And about the ninth hour Jesus cried with a loud voice, saying, "Eli, Eli, lama sabachthani: that is to say, My God, my God, why hast thou forsaken me" (Matthew 27:46)? God will never leave us or forsake us but sometimes circumstances are so dark, we feel forsaken. You can feel forsaken during the midst of a divorce, an infirmity that has plagued you for years, loneliness, or some other trial you have endured, but God will use it for His Glory and also to bless and encourage others.

BEHOLD THE BRIDEGROOM COMETH

The midnight cry of the Exodus was a cry of grief and despair but the greatest midnight cry came to announce the arrival of the Bridegroom. Jesus Christ, the Bridegroom, is coming for a bride that has been tried and purified in the fire. When you study the scriptures it is apparent that the coming of the Bridegroom will not be at a time that is convenient to the believer. It also appears that many believers will not be ready when the bridegroom comes. Matthew 25:6 reveals to us the hour that the bridegroom will come and that hour will be at midnight. This does not mean He will return at 12am. It is symbolic of a time of gross darkness that will be upon the earth. Midnight is not a time of ease and comfort and that is why many will not be ready to meet the bridegroom when He returns. In Matthew 24 Jesus told His disciples of the affliction and the deception that will arise in the last days. He instructed them to be watchful because only God knows the exact day of His return. When we look at the condition of the world today it is evident we are living in the last days and the midnight season is fast approaching. The question begs to be asked. "Will you be ready when the Bridegroom cometh?"

Some of the conditions described by Jesus about future events are the rising of many false prophets who will deceive many. He said iniquity will abound, and the love of many shall wax cold. A friend shared a story with me of a homeless man that came to the aid of a woman that was being beaten by a man. The man pulled a knife and stabbed the homeless man. Many people passed by the man bleeding on the ground and they did nothing. My friend told me that someone actually took a picture with her camera phone but did nothing to help the man. I heard a horrific story a few days ago of a young man who cut his mother's head off and was walking around with it in a bag. In describing the condition of men in the last days Paul declared to his disciple Timothy, *"This know also, that in the last days perilous times shall come. For men shall be lovers of their own* selves, covetous, boasters, proud, blasphemers, disobedient to parents, unthankful, unholy, without natural affection, truce breakers, false accusers, incontinent, fierce, despisers of those that are good. Traitors, heady, high minded, lovers of pleasures more than lovers of God; Having a form of godliness, but denying the power thereof: from such turn away" (2 Timothy 3:1-4). We need not be ignorant of the season of the return of the Bridegroom; all that is needed is the ability to discern the manifestation of the behavior patterns Paul spoke of.

When I think I have heard it all there is always something else that is more shocking than the previous story. Jesus said the people that will be saved will be the people that can endure to the end. The Greek word for endure is *hupomeno* and it means to stay under, to bear trials, to have fortitude and to be able to suffer. With the unbalanced prosperity messages believers have been subject to over the years I wonder how many will be able to endure to the end.

The midnight cry represents the abrupt coming of the bridegroom. In Matthew 25 Jesus tells the story of the ten virgins which took their lamps and went to meet the bridegroom. Five of them were wise and five of them were foolish. The foolish virgins had no oil in their lamps when they went to meet the Bridegroom. When you meditate on the fact that they had lamps without oil and it was night, you understand why the Bible says they were foolish. Please take note of the fact they were virgins. In his manual titled, The Call of the Bride, My pastor, Dr. Samuel Greene wrote this concerning Matthew 25: 1-13. "The kingdom of heaven is the kingdom of God's people. It is made up of virgins, or righteous people, all Christians. I believe the lamps are their souls. The Bible says the light (lamp) of the body is the eye, speaking of the soul. The first thing we notice about this scripture is that the Body of Christ is divided in half, fifty percent being foolish and fifty percent wise. A general look at the church will confirm this as we see that at least half are not given to running after Jesus wholeheartedly. There is always a remnant who are serious and willing to commit themselves. Dr Greene goes on to say, "These foolish Christians took no oil. What does this mean? Oil in the scriptures represents the Holy Ghost, God's anointing or His presence. So these Christians did not take, or cultivate the Holy Ghost, the anointing, or the manifest presence of God in their lives. Some are unwillingly ignorant, but we are referring to those who have heard or seen the baptism of the Holy Ghost and have criticized or rejected it, doing so to their own shame. The wise have the Holy Ghost and have cultivated His manifest presence in their lives."

When the Bible speaks of virgins it is not speaking of sinners but believers. Dr. Greene says, *"I cannot stand it when commentators say that the five foolish virgins are not Christians. The first verse of the chapter says the kingdom of heaven is like 10 virgins. There are no unsaved people in the kingdom of heaven."* It is amazing that although they were virgins they missed the marriage because of a lack of oil in their vessels. I concur with Dr. Greene's conclusion that they did not cultivate a relationship with the Holy Ghost. The believer is a vessel chosen by God to be filled with His precious Holy Spirit. The Apostle Paul told the Corinthians, "But we have this treasure in earthen vessels, that the excellency of the power may be of God, and not of us" (2 Corinthians 4:7). Although God has given the believer a treasure in their earthen vessel, the believer must continue to allow the Lord to mold and to shape the vessel so the light will continue to shine. It is obvious that the foolish virgins had allowed their oil to run out and were unprepared for the return of the bridegroom at midnight.

Do not allow the cares of this world to cause the light of the Holy Ghost to dim in you. We must constantly allow the Lord to trim our wicks and to cleanse us, so the oil of the Holy Ghost can burn bright. Our salvation is secure in Him but if we expect to enter through the marital door we must allow the light of the Holy Ghost to shine. It is not easy for us when the Lord is working to cleanse our vessel but it is absolutely necessary. Jeremiah said, *"Then I went down to the potter's house, and, behold, he wrought a work on the wheels. And the vessel that he made of clay was marred in the hand of the potter: so he made it again another vessel, as seemed good to the potter to make it" (Jeremiah 18:4).* God is the potter and we are the clay that was marred by sin. He has us on the potter's wheel reshaping us into vessels of honor. If we expect to become new vessels, then we must stay on the potter's wheel and allow Him to work the clay until the imperfections are removed.

The bridegroom did not come right away so the wise and the foolish virgins slept. At midnight the cry was made that the bridegroom

FIDEL M. DONALDSON

had arrived and they should go out to meet him. All believers will hear the cry to go and meet the Bridegroom, but some will not go in with Him because of a lack of readiness. All ten virgins arose and trimmed their lamps. The Greek word for trimmed is *kosmeo* and it means to put in proper order, to decorate, to adorn or to garnish. The Holy Ghost was sent by the Father to aid in the sanctification of the Christian. Through the sanctification process He puts our lives in order, and decorates and adorns us in preparation for our marriage to the Bridegroom. He supplies the oil that keeps our lamps burning, but we have to trim our wicks. If we do not allow Him to do His work in us we will not be ready when the Bridegroom returns.

The ten virgins were getting their lamps ready but unfortunately the 5 foolish ones were missing the most important ingredient which is the oil. There are many believers that have the outward adorning of religion, there are many churches that are decorated and the services are very timely and orderly but they are missing the most important ingredient and that is the moving of the Holy Ghost. They are adorned and decorated with the best religious trappings, they look good on the outside but the oil is missing so there is not light. It is not enough to busy ourselves with religious church chores to the exclusion of our daily devotion to the Lord Jesus. My pastor always tells us, "We should not be so busy doing the work of the Lord that we neglect the Lord of the work." The dichotomy between believers devoted to the important spiritual things and the ones overloaded with the cares of this world can be seen in the activities of Martha and her sister Mary when Jesus visited their home. Mary sat at the feet of Jesus while Martha was troubled about the serving. Martha's serving was not a bad thing but it was not the best thing, because when Jesus is in the house all chores must cease and we must bow at His feet and glean from His words. David said God's word was a light unto his path and a lamp unto his feet. The light of the Holy Ghost works in tandem with the Word of God to prepare the believer to meet the bridegroom.

The light of the foolish virgins had gone out because it was not replenished. A constant yielding to the Holy Ghost will cause His presence to be replenished in the life of the believer. We have to use our oil in-order to see in this dark world so we must endeavor to replenish it. The tarrying of the bridegroom has caused some believers to become slothful and lukewarm. "Jesus calls believers the light of the world." Our light comes from the oil of the Holy Ghost and it is given to us by the Lord so men will see our good works and glorify our Heavenly Father. When our light is not shining God does not get glory.

The foolish virgins wanted the wise to give them some of their oil but they refused. Every believer will have to have their own relationship with the Holy Ghost. A spiritual relationship cannot be bought it must be cultivated through much perseverance. We cannot afford to live our lives as if the Bridegroom will not return. When the foolish virgins went to purchase more oil the bridegroom came and the ones that were ready went into the marriage with Him and the door was shut. As believers we must prepare ourselves for the coming of our Lord, because once He comes we will not enter the bridal chamber if we are not prepared. Once the door is shut there is nothing we can do to open it. At some point the foolish virgins returned and asked the Lord to open the door but he responded by saying, "I know you not." When the Bridegroom said He never knew them He was telling them they had no intimacy with Him.

Hosea 2:16 speaks of a people who will call the Lord Ishi which means my husband. The five foolish virgins never spent time at His feet gleaning from the words that proceeded from His mouth. They went through the religious motions but never gave themselves wholeheartedly to the Holy Ghost. They will not lose their salvation because they are Christians, but they will not attain to the prize of the high calling in Jesus Christ that Paul spoke about to the in Philippians 3:14. They represent the company that will be on the outside calling Him Lord, but those who are allowed to enter the bridal chamber will be able to call Him Ishi.

The bride will be the over comers, they are the ones who are able to press beyond distractions and the things that are behind. They reach forth and lay hold of the things that are ahead of them. They emulate Jesus by setting their faces like flints. They keep their eyes on the prize. Like Jesus they are able to focus on the joy that is set before them. The Joy is the place of intimacy with the Bridegroom. They spent untold amount of hours preparing for His return. They sacrificed things the foolish were not willing to give up in-order to know Him intimately. They gave themselves wholeheartedly to the things of God, while the foolish virgins were satisfied with the superficial and the superfluous. All 10 virgins had knowledge of and a desire to meet Him but the thing that separated them was their preparation. They all had lamps that were burning when they went out to meet him but his tarrying and subsequent return further gave evidence of the things that separated them. The priests were never to allow the lamp in the temple to go out. It is time for an oil check. You have traveled hundreds of thousands of miles on this journey and you might be low on oil. Your engine will seize up if you attempt to drive without oil.

THE BAPTISM OF THE HOLY GHOST

The ministry of the Holy Ghost is a very important one and that is why I believe we cannot have enough teaching on His ministry to the body of Christ. Once we are saved it is His ministry in our lives that helps guide us and comfort us in the midnight seasons of life. Salvation represents the new birth and once we are birthed into the Kingdom of God the Holy Ghost comes to live in us. Some people have houses that they live in only in the summer. There is a subsequent baptism which God gives as a gift and allows us to be filled with the Holy Ghost. There is a difference between the person who comes to visit for awhile and the person who comes to live with us. Many people might not believe in the baptism of the Holy Ghost but the scriptural evidence is irrefutable. For John truly baptized with water; but ye shall be baptized with the Holy Ghost not many days hence. (Acts 1:5)

The disciples had been with Jesus, they went out in the power of the Spirit but the baptism of the Holy Ghost was not received while Jesus was with them. When Jesus told them that He had to go away, their hearts were filled with sorrow, and rightfully so. He told them it was expedient for them that He go away because if He stayed the Comforter would not be sent to them. The Comforter is the Holy Ghost. The Greek word for expedient is sumphero and it means to be advantageous or profitable. It is derived from the word sun which is

102

a primary preposition denoting union with or together, and the word phero, a primary verb which means to bear, bring forth, to carry or to endure. When Jesus was on the earth He had the Holy Ghost without measure.

Acts 2:1 describes what took place when the disciples were assembled together in the upper room on the day of Pentecost. "And they were all filled with the Holy Ghost, and began to speak with other tongues, as the Spirit gave them utterance." When Peter spoke to the devout men he said, "Repent, and be baptized every one of you in the name of Jesus Christ for the remission of sins, and ye shall receive the gift of the Holy Ghost *(Acts 2:38).* Repentance allows the Blood of Jesus to give us remission of sins, but it also paves the way for us to receive the baptism of the Holy Ghost. It is not for a certain period for Peter went on to say, For the promise is unto you, and to your children, and to all that are afar off, even as many as the Lord our God shall call" (Acts 2:39). *Acts 4:31 says* "And when they had prayed, the place was shaken where they were assembled together; and they were all filled with the Holy Ghost, and they spake the word of God with boldness." Those were not unbelievers who were praying because the prayers of unbelievers cannot shake anything. Those were believers but apparently they needed to be filled with the Holy Ghost to speak the word with boldness. There is a plethora of other scriptures I can quote to show that after the born again experience a believer still needs to ask God for the gift of the Holy Ghost, but I will give you one more. "Now when the apostles which were at Jerusalem heard that Samaria had received the word of God, they sent unto them Peter and John: Who, when they were come down, prayed for them, that they might receive the Holy Ghost: (For as yet he was fallen upon none of them: they were baptized in the name of the Lord Jesus. Then laid they their hands on them, and they received the Holy Ghost" *(Acts 8:14-17).*

Those believers had received the word, they were baptized in the name of the Lord Jesus but they had not received the gift of the Holy Ghost. There are many believers sitting in churches today who have received the word, many were baptized in the name of the Lord Jesus but have not received the gift of the Holy Ghost because they were taught that they were filled with the power of the Holy Ghost when they were birthed into the Kingdom of God. Search the scriptures for yourself for it is there in plain sight. Who are you going to believe? Are you going to take the word of a man, or are you going to believe the Word of God? Let God be true and every man be a liar. Look at the life of Peter before he received the baptism of the Holy Ghost and after. He walked with Jesus and saw the miracles. But when Jesus was arrested he stood by the fire outside of the home of the high priest and cussed someone out when they accused him of being a follower of Jesus. Jesus knew Peter would deny Him. On one occasion when Jesus taught His disciples about being servants he spoke these words to Peter, "Simon Simon, behold, Satan hath desired to have you, that he may sift you as wheat: But I have prayed for thee, that thy faith fail not: and when thou art converted, strengthen thy brethren" (Luke 22:31-32). Simon responded by telling Jesus he was ready to go with him, both into prison, and to death. Jesus told him, "I tell thee Peter, the cock shall not crow this day, before that thou shalt thrice deny that thou knowest me" (Luke 22:34). After receiving the baptism of the Holy Ghost Peter is standing with boldness preaching the Word of God. When was he converted? He was converted when he received the baptism of the Holy Ghost.

The five foolish virgins slumbered while the Bridegroom tarried. Revelation 19:7-8 is a great companion scripture to Matthew 25:6. *"Let us be glad and rejoice, and give honour to him: for the marriage of the Lamb is come, and his wife hath made herself ready. And to her was granted that she should be arrayed in fine linen, clean and white: for the fine linen is the righteousness of saints."* "Note the fact John said his wife hath made herself ready." The Holy Ghost will not force Himself on us; we have to yield to Him so He will make us ready. We have to turn our backs on the things which hinder the preparation process. Fine linen is a symbol of moral purity, righteousness. (Genesis 41:42). When Joseph stood before Pharaoh after being prepared by his experience in the pit, Potiphar's house, and the prison, Pharaoh showed his approval by taking his ring off his hand and placing it on Joseph's hand, and arrayed him in vestures of fine linen, and put a gold chain about his neck. When Jesus told His disciples to tarry at Jerusalem until they be endued with power from on high, the Greek word for tarry is kathizo and it means to set, sit down or to settle. The

Greek word for endued is, "enduo and it means to array, to clothe; to invest with clothing." I do not believe the foolish virgins took time to sit or settle in the presence of the Lord until He arrayed them in the vesture of the fine linen of the Holy Ghost.

Many believers are clothed with the garment of religion. Many churches and many Christians look the same and have similar Church activities and order of service but when Jesus returns there will be a separation because the distinction between His Church and the pseudo church will be clear. Believers who are clothed in the vesture of the Holy Ghost, the ones whose lives are radiating the light of the Holy Ghost, the ones who have trimmed their wicks and replenished their supply of oil will be allowed in the bridal chamber.

The Lord knows we need rest but we cannot spend so much time in slumber and sleep that we become oblivious to the fact that our lamps have run out of oil. No matter how long we have to wait for the return of the Bridegroom we must occupy ourselves with a Kingdom agenda while we wait. We must not become weary in well doing; we must continue to be active in the reading, the studying of the Word of God, and yielding to the Holy Ghost. The more we yield to Him the more oil He releases into our souls. We have to be careful not to forsake the assembling of ourselves together. There are a lot of people who feel they do not need to attend a local church and that is a dangerous deception. When we assemble ourselves in the local church we must be steadfast in learning the Word. Church services are so programmed nowadays they are more personality driven than Spirit led. We have to come to the local church with a mindset to worship the Lord until a prophetic anointing is released. We have to have a mindset and an expectation to receive a proceeding word that will exhort, encourage and build us up.

There is a story told in the book of Acts about some disciples gathering together on a Sunday to break bread. The Apostle Paul was at the meeting and was preparing to depart on the following day. The Apostle ministered to them until midnight. The Bible says, and there were many lights in the upper chamber, where they were gathered together. And there sat in a window a certain young man named Eutychus, being fallen into a deep sleep: and as Paul was long preaching, he sunk down with sleep and fell down from the third loft, and was taken up dead" (Acts 20:7-9) Although the Apostle preached long I do not believe his sermon was boring. We have to condition ourselves to stay alert during the preaching of the Word of God even if the sermon is long. If we are caught in a deep sleep at midnight our life can be taken from us.

WORK WHILE IT IS DAY

Jesus has given us work to do in this earth and each one of us will be held accountable when we stand before him. We cannot keep our eyes on others; we must focus on the work He has called up to perform. It is very easy to be distracted by the cares of this life and forget the kingdom assignment we have received from the Lord. He has given us authority to do search and destroy missions against the kingdom of darkness and we must walk in that authority. Reader, you need to know what your particular job for the Lord is and you need to work while it is day.

Jesus is very serious about the work He has given us to do and He has told us in the scriptures what will happen if we are slothful and derelict in our duties. *"And it came to pass, that, as they went in the way, a certain man said unto him, Lord, I will follow thee whithersoever thou goest. And Jesus said unto him, Foxes have holes, and birds of the air have nests; but the Son of man hath not where to lay his head. And he said unto another, Follow me. But he said, Lord, suffer me first to go and bury my father. Jesus said unto him, Let the dead bury their dead: but go thou and preach the kingdom of God. And another also said, Lord, I will follow thee; but let me first go bid them farewell, which are at home at my house. And Jesus said unto him, No man, having put his hand to the plough, and looking back, is fit for the kingdom of God. (Luke 9: 57-62).* The Greek word for fit is euthetos, and it means well placed, suitable or to make ready. Believers in Jesus Christ are called to be light and salt. Light dispels darkness and salt preserves. Jesus is calling His disciples to a willingness to forsake all for the work of the kingdom. Jesus said, "Whosoever he be of you that forsaketh not all that he hath, he cannot be my disciple. Salt is good but if the salt have lost his savour, wherewith shall it be seasoned? It is neither fit for the land, nor yet for the dunghill; but men cast it out. He that hath ears to hear, let him hear. (Luke 14:33-35)

When religious leaders persecuted Jesus and tried to kill Him He responded by saying, "My Father worketh hitherto, and I work" (John 5:17). It is important that we exercise our authority and do the work God has called us to. The devil will attempt to break down our minds and physically exhaust us so we fall into a state of slumber so we must not be ignorant of his devices. Deception is one of his greatest weapons.

It is hard to believe that a believer would be unaware about their light not shining, but please keep in mind that the Lord is not speaking to sinners here. There will be believers that will have the door shut on them because of a lack of preparation. Jesus reminds believers to watch because we do not know the day or the hour when He will return. As said previously, we do not know the day nor the hour but we do know the season. That season will be at midnight. Concerning the children of Issachar the Bible says, *"And of the children of Issachar, which were men that had understanding of the times" (1 Chronicles 32a).* It will be a season of gross darkness on the earth. Only believers with the light of the Holy Ghost shining will be able to be recognized by the Lord. Because the children of Issachar had understanding of the times they were able to know what Israel should do. We need men and women of God who are yielded to the Holy Ghost. Men and women that are able to instruct the body on what they should do in the midnight hour. As the world becomes darker and darker, people will run to and fro in search of light. Many will be deceived into thinking right is wrong and wrong is right, but many will come to a realization of their need for a savior. We have to be able to present the true savior to them because the Bible tells us that false prophets will deceive many.

MIDNIGHT: WATCH AND PRAY

Jesus instructs the believer to watch and pray since we do not know the time of His return. "For the Son of man is as a man taking a far journey, who left his house, and gave authority to his servants, and to every man his work, and commanded the porter to watch. Watch ye therefore: for ye know not when the master of the house cometh, at even, or at midnight, or at the cockcrowing, or in the morning: Lest coming suddenly he find you sleeping" (Mark 13:34-36). The coming of the Lord will be sudden; it is likened unto a thief coming in the night. The Lord knows we have to sleep, so He is not referring to our normal sleep in this particular passage. He is talking about His servants that slumber and become slothful when they should be watching and working. The Greek word Mark used for watch is gregoreuo (pronounced gray-gor-yoo-o); it means to keep awake, to be vigilant. The English name "Gregory" comes from this Greek word translated "watch."

The principle of the watch is very important and there are a plethora of scriptures that deal with it. The word watch represents a division of the night. In the Old Testament the night was divided into three watches; the first watch (Lam 2:19), the midnight watch (Judges 7:19), and the morning watch (Exodus 14:24; 1 Samuel 11:11). By New Testament times the Jews were following the Roman custom of dividing the night into four watches: evening, midnight, cockcrow, and morning (Mark 13:35).

There are many scriptural references to the duties of watchmen who were appointed to give warning when an enemy approached. Ezekiel was called by God to be a watchman on the wall. His assignment was very important. It was so important that God told Ezekiel that the blood of the wicked would be required of his hand if he did not warn them to flee wickedness. God warns the watchman when danger is coming and he has to warn the people. If the watchman is asleep he will not be able to sound the trumpet when an attack is launched. Warning comes before destruction so when destruction comes it is because the warning was not heeded. The phrase connecting the dots was used a great deal after the tragedy of September 11, when terrorists flew planes into various buildings in the United States.

The agencies that were supposed detect and decipher pertinent information failed to share the information with each other. Sophisticated technology can aid but will never totally replace human effort and ingenuity. The United States has spy satellites, sophisticated telecommunications systems which allow our government to listen to cell phone conversations people are having in countries that are far away. Once information is received that there is a threat, the information has to be disseminated to the appropriate agencies who will take action to neutralize the threat. A chain is only as strong as its weakest link, so, if the CIA and the FBI are not communicating with each other and with other agencies, there is a weakness in the chain and the chain will eventually break, it broke on September 11.

The watchmen God has set in the body of Christ must be alert; they must be able to hear the voice of the Lord and give warning when danger is coming. They must be able to discern the diabolical plot of the spiritual terrorist seeking to plant demonic bombs. When we allow ourselves to be divided there will be a break in the chain and an opening for the enemy to penetrate our defense.

THE FIRST WATCH

"Woe to them that are at ease in Zion" (Amos 6:1). Zion is Judah and Judah means praise. Woe is a form of judgment and God pronounced it on Judah and Israel because of their indifference to His word. God is serious about His word and He will deal with us based on our obedience to the word. Chapter 2 of the book of Lamentations tells of God's anger at sin and introduces us to the first watch. In speaking of Zion and Israel the Lord declares, "Her gates are sunk into the ground; he hath destroyed and broken her bars: her king and her princes are among the Gentiles: the law is no more; her prophets also find no vision from the Lord." (Lamentations 2:9). Gates are symbolic of entrance, power and authority. The royal line is backslidden because they are among the Gentiles. The worst part of their condition is the fact that there is lawlessness and "no vision from the Lord." The Hebrew word for vision as it used here is Chazown; it is the same word used in Proverbs 29:18. Where there is no vision, the people perish: but he that keepeth the law, happy is he." As mentioned earlier, vision is not the ability to see optically, but it is a dream, revelation, or oracle. The prophets were not able to get a revelation or an oracle from the Lord and this caused the people to perish and fall into lawlessness. In verse 19 God tells the people to,

"Arise, cry out in the night: in the beginning of the watches pour out thine heart like water before the face of the Lord: lift up thy hands toward him for the life of thy young children that faint for hunger in the top of every street." The night season represents a time of despair and God wanted His people to arise and cry out to Him in repentance. He wanted them to do it in the beginning of the watches, because the watches represent the division of the night and as the watches progressed the night became darker. The watchman has to discern the hour and warn the people.

THE SECOND AND THIRD WATCH

Blessed are those servants, whom the lord when he cometh shall find watching: verily I say unto you, that he shall gird himself, and make them to sit down to meat, and will come forth and serve them. And if he shall come in the second watch, or come in the third watch, and find them so, blessed are those servants. (Luke 12:37-38). The Bible tells us to serve the Lord, and rightfully so. This passage of scripture in Luke is absolutely amazing because it tells us the blessing we will receive if we are diligent in watching when the Lord returns. Jesus will make us sit down to meat and He will serve us. Can you imagine Jesus serving us in the kingdom? The Greek word used in that passage for serve is diakoneo and it means to be an attendant, to host. Jesus will have a table prepared for us where we will sit down to dine and He will be the one doing the serving. It is a blessing to know that the people who will receive this great honor and blessing will be the servants. People who are looking to be served, people that are pushing titles, and people who are not laboring in the vineyard will not be at the table. This is why Jesus placed an emphasis on serving when the disciples were indignant over the fact that the mother of Zebedee's children asked Jesus if they could sit on His right and left in the kingdom. We should never forget the individual who came to the marriage supper without the proper garments. He was bound and cast into outer darkness. "For many are called, but few are chosen" (Mathew 22:11). Few are chosen to sit and eat meat with King Jesus and receive the blessing of being served by the King, because few chose to serve the King while here on earth. Many are more interested in the outward show of religion, than in solidifying their relationship with Him. They will hear the dreadful words, "I never knew you: depart from me, ye that work iniquity" (Matthew 7:23)

THE FOURTH WATCH

"And in the fourth watch of the night Jesus went unto them, walking on the sea" (Matthew 14:25). In the scriptures the number four is symbolic of creation and the creature. On page 60 of his book Biblical Mathematics: Keys to Scripture Numerics, Evangelist Ed. F. Vallowe wrote, "Four is the number of CREATION and marks GOD'S creative works. It is the signature of the world." In bringing life to the dry bones God told the prophet Ezekiel to call the wind that comes from the four winds. Concerning the return of Jesus, Matthew 24:31 declares, "And He shall send his angels with a great sound of a trumpet, and they shall gather together his elect from the four winds, from one end of heaven to the other." The material creation was finished on the fourth day. In the first and second chapters of Genesis, in the record of creation, the word creature is found four times. In Revelation 5:13 the creatures in four different places ascribe four works of praise to the Father and to Christ.

We see the creative power of the Lord Jesus when he raised Lazarus from the grave. When He received the news that Lazarus was sick, Jesus said, "This sickness is not unto death, but for the glory of God, that the Son of God might be glorified. He tarried where He was for two more days and arrived on the fourth day when Lazarus was in the tomb. When he raised Lazarus from the dead he performed a creative miracle.

When Jesus comes in the fourth watch of the night He comes to perform creative miracles. Prior to coming to His disciples in the fourth watch of the night Jesus had fed the five thousand. After the feeding He constrained His disciples to get into a ship, and to go before him to the other side, while he sent the multitude away. The multitude was sent away because only disciples are going to go through the storm to meet Jesus. The multitude's main interest is, miracles, the fish the barley loaves, and not His presence. Disciples want to be with Jesus even if it means they must sail through tempestuous seas. Why do you think the multitude pack an auditorium when there is a prophetic service, or a concert or when their favorite motivational preacher comes to town, but they will not show up in great numbers when there is a service on prayer, or evangelism? To be quite honest, you do not hear about many conferences on prayer or evangelism. As stated previously, people will pack stadiums to hear how blessed they are going to be and how they are going to prosper.

When He sent the multitude away and the disciples were in the ship heading to the other side, Jesus went up into a mountain apart to pray. "And when the evening was come He was there alone." The evening represents a time when darkness is coming on. There will be some times in our walk with the Lord when we will find ourselves alone. We will not be out of God's presence but will be alone in terms of human companionship. The prophet Jeremiah declared, *"I sat not in the assembly of the mockers, nor rejoiced; I sat alone because of thy hand: for thou hast filled me with indignation" (Jeremiah 15:17)*. While Jesus was praying alone in the evening the ship in which the disciples traveled was in the midst of the sea being tossed with waves: "for the wind was contrary." Jesus came walking on the sea in the fourth watch of the night and when the disciples saw him they were troubled. They cried out for fear thinking it was a spirit. Jesus told them to "Be of good cheer; it is I; be not afraid."

We have to be able to discern the presence of the Lord in the midst of the boisterous seas upon which we journey. Fear will cause our vision to be blurred. Fear ought not to cause us not to see Jesus coming to our rescue in the storm. The disciples were troubled and gripped with fear. Disciples need to have peace in the midst of the storm. Sometimes the thing we see in the storm is the answer God has sent to solve the problem, but we have to be able to recognize it and not be afraid to embrace it. "God hath not given us the spirit of fear but of love power, and of love and of a sound mind" (2 Timothy 1:7). Paul does not speak of a spirit of fear he says, "The spirit of fear." It is a particular spirit that attacks the disciples in their midnight crisis to destroy them. The spirit of fear is from the devil but God counteracts it by giving miracle working power to His disciples. The Greek word for power here is dunamis. It is ability, might, strength; it is miraculous power. When the apostle used the word "sound," it is the Greek word sophronismos (pronounced so-fron-is-mos); it means discipline, self-control. Disciples are individuals who have disciplined themselves, individuals who have yielded to the Holy Ghost and exercise self-control. Now we see why Jesus sent the multitude away after feeding them. They would not have had the discipline and the self-control to go through the storm. There would have been pandemonium if they were on the rough seas. The disciplined ones are the ones who will endure the midnight trials; they will feel the pressure of the storm but they will not quit because they know Jesus will eventually show up and calm the storm.

We have to expect a miraculous visitation from the Lord in the midst of our storm. There is no storm that is so great that Jesus cannot calm it. If you are dealing with a storm at the present time be of good cheer, because Jesus is coming in the fourth watch of the night. He is coming to work a miracle for you. Do not allow the spirit of fear to cause you to slip.

Once the disciples realized it was Jesus coming to them walking on the water, Peter asked Jesus to "bid me to come unto thee on the water, and he said come." That is what Jesus is saying to His disciples who can discern His presence in the fourth watch of the night, the disciples that need peace in the midst of the storm, Jesus says, "come." Come and be healed, delivered, and set free. Come all you that are heavy laden, and yoked with burdens, come and receive rest at the feet of Jesus. Peter got out of the ship and started walking on the water towards Jesus, but when he saw the boisterous wind he was afraid, and began to sink.

We are on a journey that is taking us to Jesus and we will need to set our face like flint because there are many bumps in the road. Keep looking to Jesus the author and the finisher of your faith. He will turn the stumbling blocks into stepping stones. When you experience a set back do not take a step back because Jesus is working on your comeback. Hallelujah!!!

As Peter sank he cried out, "Lord save me." This has to be the cry of every person that is sinking. The saint, the sinner and the backslider must cry out to Jesus in the time of trouble. Fear will cause the disciple to take their eyes off of Jesus at times because of boisterous winds, but call on Jesus and He will answer. The backslider thought the grass was greener on the other side until he went over there and found out there was quick sand beneath it. All the back slider needed to do was cry out to King Jesus and say, "Lord save me." The sinner is definitely sinking in the muck and the mire of sin but he need only cry to Jesus, because He hears the repentant cry of the sinner. When Peter cried out "Lord, save me" The Bible declares, *"And immediately Jesus stretched forth his hand, and caught him, and said unto him, O thou of little faith, wherefore didst thou doubt."* Remember what Paul and Silas did at midnight? They prayed and sang praises unto God. Do you remember what happened afterwards? They received their breakthrough, a suddenly and an immediately. Never forget to pray and lift up praises unto God at midnight when the darkness has reached its apex. Midnight may seem like a long time; it might appear as if the light will never shine, but remember, when midnight arrives so does the new day, and if you can hold on to the unchanging hand of Jesus, the darkness will dissipate and the light will begin to shine. Take some time now and pray, take some time right now and lift up praise unto to your Father in Heaven. Give Him a new song, give Him a new praise, give him midnight praise and expect the foundations of the prison to be shaken, expect the prison door to open and the bands to be loosed, expect a miracle.

You are one praise away from your next miracle. He inhabits the praises of His people and that is why when Paul and Silas praised He manifested in the prison because His habitation is your praise. It does not make a difference that your praise is coming from the confines of a literal prison because that is exactly where Paul and Silas were at midnight. If you are in prison now just praise Him, and He will be in the prison with you. Paul and Silas understood what David meant in Psalm 34 when he declared, *"I will bless the LORD at all times: his praise shall continually be in my mouth. My soul shall make her boast in the LORD: the humble shall hear thereof, and be glad. O magnify the LORD with me, and let us exalt his name together. I sought the LORD, and he heard me, and delivered me from all my fears. They looked unto him, and were lightened: and their faces were not ashamed. This poor man cried, and the LORD heard him, and saved him out of all his troubles.*

The angel of the LORD encampeth round about them that fear him, and delivereth them.

David used the Hebrew word barak for bless and it means to kneel; to bless God as an act of adoration. He said he would bless Him at all times, that means in good times and in bad. The soul is the center of the human will, intellect, and emotions. David said his soul would boast in the Lord. He used the Hebrew word halal for boast and it means to shine, to make a show, to be clamorously foolish, to rave, celebrate and to stultify. We get our word hallelujah from the word halal. We do not need a cute praise in the midnight hour; we should not be bound by the opinions of people who try to intimidate us when we make our boast in the Lord. We might look foolish to them but God is pleased with it. When David danced before the Lord with all his might, his wife Michal accused him of being "as one of the vain fellows shamelessly that uncover themselves, but he told her, "It was before the LORD." We do not praise to please people and we should not hold back the halal praise because of people. Michal did not understand that praise was a garment. God gives us the garment of praise for the spirit of heaviness. We have to halal God in the midnight hour and when He delivers us into the light we have to halal him some more. We are in a global recession right now but my modus operandi is to halal going into every situation and halal coming out.

David said the humble would hear and be glad. The only people that are bothered by radical praise are people who are not humble. The Hebrew word for humble is *anav* and it means meek and lowly. Jesus said we should learn of him because He is meek and lowly in heart and we will find rest for our souls. David's soul had rest because it boasted in the LORD. When our souls boast in the Lord Jesus it will find rest. David exhorted the people to magnify and exalt the name of the LORD. He used the Hebrew word *gadal* for magnify and it means to be or make large in body, mind, estate or honor. It also means to boast, advance, exceed and to bring up. There are times when our minds will be stressed, oppressed and depressed by a midnight crisis; this is the time when we should make our souls boast in the Lord. We have to make ourselves lift up a halal praise unto Him. When we do that He will deliver us. David used the Hebrew word *darash* for sought and it means to follow, pursue, search; it means to inquire diligently to seek or ask specifically to worship.

Hebrews 11:6 declares, "But without faith it is impossible to please him: for he that cometh to God must believe that he is, and that he is a rewarder of them that diligently seek him." It is not enough to rest on the fact that we believe in God because the Apostle James declared, *"Thou believest there is one God; thou doest well: the devils also believe, and tremble" (James 2:19)*. We have to go from mere belief to radical pursuit. The Greek word used for seek in Hebrews 11:6 is the Greek word ekzeteo, and it means to search out, investigate, crave, to demand, to enquire carefully, diligently, and to worship. Is that not amazing when you compare boast in Psalm 34 and seek in Hebrews 11:6. This is why scripture must be studied line upon line, and precept upon precept. Here is something just as fascinating; The Greek word used for seek in Matthew 6:33 is zeteo and of course it means to worship, to enquire or desire God.

Halal praise and worship are keys that will unlock blessings for us, especially in the midnight hour. The devil and his demons will be confused because when they have thrown everything at us including the kitchen sink, we will give God radical praise and worship. The darker the night, the more we praise. Murmuring brings darkness but praise and worship brings light, so praise Him until the light begins to shine.

Chapter 6
IT'S MIDNIGHT: YOU CAN MAKE IT ON BROKEN PIECES

The church of Jesus Christ can be likened unto a ship sailing through tempestuous seas. Jesus is the Captain of our ship and He is able to navigate the ship so it can reach its destination. The roughness of the seas will mean the ship will take some hits but when the seas become rough you must abide in the ship because your destination is secure. It will reach its destination because our captain has authority over the winds and the waves. God allows the ship to go through tempestuous seas in order to strengthen our faith and our trust in Him.

Matthew records a story when Jesus and his disciples went into a boat and there arose a great tempest in the sea that caused the boat to be covered by the waves. Amazingly Jesus was asleep in the back of the boat. When Jesus is in the boat you can rest because He gives you peace in the midst of the storm. The disciples were panicked by the height of the waves and asked Jesus to save them because they were going to perish. My question is, "How can you perish when Jesus is in the Boat?" Jesus asked them why they were fearful and accused them of having little faith. "Then He arose, and rebuked the winds and the sea; and there was a great calm" *(Matthew 8:26).* The disciples wanted to know what manner of man He was that even the winds and the waves obeyed Him. He is the God man, the word that became flesh, the one that created all things. He created the winds and the waves and they were subject to Him because the created thing can never be greater than He which created it. When the midnight seas are rough, when the waves are about to overtake you, trust in Jesus, for He is the captain of your salvation.

IT IS WELL

Losing a child has to be one of the most heart wrenching things any parent has to deal with, especially an only child. When the Shunamite woman found out that her son was dead she hastened to the prophet Elisha because he spoke the prophetic word that caused her barren womb to be fruitful. When Elisha saw her afar off he told his servant Gehazi to run to her and ask her three questions. "Is it well with thee? Is it well with thy husband? Is it well with the child? And she answered, *"it is well" (2 Kings 4:26)*. It takes a strong man or woman to say, "It is well" when they have lost a child. There is no way to comprehend the pain and the heartache that type of loss causes; concerning Jesus the Bible says, "it pleased God to bruise him" (Isaiah 53:10). Isaiah said he was wounded for our transgression and he was bruised for our iniquities. God loved us so much that he allowed Jesus to be bruised for us. If you have suffered the loss of a child or some other loved one, remember that God sent his beloved son to die on the cross for us.

The hymn *"It Is Well With My Soul"* was penned by hymnist Horatio Spafford. The inspiration for the hymn came from several traumatic events in the life of Mr. Spafford. The first was the death of his only son in 1871, that incident was followed by the great Chicago fire which ruined him financially. In 1873, he was planning to travel to Europe with his family but decided to send the family because he was delayed by some business he was working on. While crossing the Atlantic the ship with his family sank after colliding with another ship. Horatio Spafford's four daughters died but his wife Anna survived and sent him the now famous telegram titled, "Saved alone." As Mr. Spafford traveled to meet his grieving wife he was inspired to write the words to the famous hymn as the ship passed near where his daughters died.

"When peace, like a river, attendeth my way,
When sorrows like sea billows roll;
Whatever my lot, Thou has taught me to say,
It is well, it is well, with my soul."

On this journey of life we will have to navigate through tough storms, and rough seas. Mr. Spafford's soul must have been anchored in Jesus for him not to drift away when he received the tragic news that his beloved daughters were drowned at sea. We have to make sure our souls are anchored in Him so we are able to stand in the midst of the storm and say, "peace be still," it is well with my soul."

The Apostle Paul had to deal with a situation where he was on a ship that was in tempestuous seas. It occurred after he stood before King Agrippa and his wife Bernice to defend himself against a judgment brought against him by the chief priests and the elders. Upon listening to Paul, Agrippa realized he had done nothing worthy of death and would have released him if he had not appealed to Caesar.

PEACE IN THE MIDST OF THE STORM

Paul and certain other prisoners were delivered to a centurion named Julius when it was time to sail to Rome. Although he was a prisoner, Julius allowed Paul to visit friends and refresh himself when they arrived at Sidon. God might not pull you out of the prison right away, but like Joseph and Paul, He will give you favor while you are there. When they departed from Sidon they sailed under Cyprus because the winds were contrary. No matter what you are facing in the midnight hour God will always give you a time of refreshing before you have to face the contrary winds. At some point they transferred to a ship of Alexandria sailing into Italy. The journey was slow and they were sailing for many days because they did not have good wind. When they arrived at a place called Fair Havens near the city of Lasea the sailing became dangerous. The Apostle said sailing was dangerous because it was the time of the fast. The fast he referred to was the Day of Atonement which fell in September/October. The sailors should have known that sailing was difficult from mid-September to mid-November, and impossible from mid-November to February. At this time Paul admonished them by saying, Sirs, *"I perceive that this voyage will be with hurt and much damage, not only of the lading and the ship, but also of our lives. Nevertheless the centurion believed the master and the owner of the ship, more than those things which were spoken by Paul" (Acts 27:10-11).* Although he was a prisoner Paul was the one with the discernment because he was the man of God.

119

The servants of the Lord Jesus Christ will find themselves in situations where the majority will be against them but they must not be intimidated because they have a word from the Lord, and that word will manifest in the midst of the rough midnight seas. When trouble comes to your door, you better have a man or woman of God in the midst who can discern and hear a word from the Lord.

There are people you will come in contact with that will not heed the warning you give them because you do not have a great deal of material things. The sons of Koreh thought they could oppose Moses because they were princes and men of renown. Naaman the Leper almost missed his healing by becoming wroth when the Prophet Elisha told him to go and wash in Jordan seven times. He thought he was being insulted because Abana and Pharpar the rivers of Damascus were much better than all the waters of Israel. He did not understand that it was the proceeding word out of the mouth of God's prophet and his willingness to obey that word that was important.

Warning comes before destruction and a haughty spirit before a fall. They ignored Paul's warning and decided to sail because Fair Havens was not commodious to winter in. They decided to try and get to Phenice to spend the winter. Phenice was a haven of Crete that was toward the South west and the North West. The distance between Fair Havens and Phenice was approximately forty miles. In the scriptures, forty is the number that symbolizes testing and probation. South is symbolic of quietness of earth; West symbolizes the closing of the day, evening, the going down of the sun. North symbolizes power, majesty, judgment, and God's throne. With these definitions you can understand the course of action described in *Acts 27:13*: "And when the south wind blew softly, supposing that they had obtained their purpose, loosing thence, they sailed close by Crete." The adversary will lull us into a false sense of security in-order to entice us to set sail. When the man or woman of God receives a word from the Lord and tells you there is danger ahead you should not move no matter how calm things look.

"But not long after, there arose against it a tempestuous wind, called Euroclydon" (Acts27:14). "For when they shall say, peace and safety; then sudden destruction cometh upon them, as travail upon a woman with child; and they shall not escape" (1 Thessalonians

120

5:3). The Apostle Paul informed the Thessalonians that he did not need to write them concerning the times and seasons because they knew the day of the Lord would come as a thief in the night. It is the people living in darkness that had to worry about sudden destruction coming upon them. The children of God are not in darkness so the day of the Lord should not overtake us like a thief. On the ship Paul was surrounded by prisoners and unbelieving shipmen who had no discernment. They obviously had no idea that there was an anointed Apostle of the Lord Jesus in their midst. They probably looked at him as another prisoner.

Despite the Apostle's warning they felt the coolness of the quiet south wind and decided to set sail and were hit by Euroclydon. It was called a tempestuous wind and that literally meant a "typhonic wind," or a typhoon. The devil is a master illusionist and he will attempt to make us launch out when it is time to stay. He attempts to entice us by making the path look smooth but we must endeavor to obey the word of the Lord and fight the temptation to go our own way. Paul wanted them to remain at Fair Havens because they had already encountered contrary winds and it was not the start of the stormy season. The life of a Christian consists of seasons of testing and seasons of breakthrough. We are either coming out of a storm or heading into one. Paul was speaking from experience when he told them not to set sail because he had previously been in three ship wrecks.

The Greek word translated "perceive" in Acts 27:10 is *theoreo* and it means "to perceive from past experience." All the experts on the ship convinced Julius to sail because Fair Havens was not a comfortable place to settle in the winter because it was too open to the winter storms. Phenice had a harbor that was more suitable for shelter. The grass always looks greener on the other side, but what benefit is it if you perish trying to get to the other side? If God tells you to stay, obey, because His grace will keep you until it is time to set sail. By ignoring the word of the Lord and listening to some experts, many people have jumped right out of the frying pan into the fire. Thank God for the experts but we need to hear a word from the Lord in the midnight hour. The experts do not get it right all the time but Almighty God never gets it wrong.

STORMS WILL MAKE US PRAY

Remember when Jonah disobeyed the word of God and boarded a ship bound for Tarshish. He attempted to flee from the presence of the Lord by going down to Joppa in order to board a ship going to Tarshish. Joppa comes from the Hebrew word yahpah which means to be fair, bright or beautiful. There is nothing fair, bright or beautiful outside of the presence of the Lord. No matter how tough the assignment, never flee from the presence of the Lord, flee to the presence of the Lord. His presence is like an ark of safety from the stormy seas. The Bible says, *"But the Lord sent out a great wind into the sea, and there was a mighty tempest in the sea, so that the ship was like to be broken" (Jonah 1:4).* Do not try to hide from God because He will wreck the ship you are hiding on to get your attention. Some of the midnight situations and the rough seas we encounter stem from the fact that we are going in a direction opposite of where God has sent us. When we fail to heed warning signs God will roughen up the seas to get us to change course. Jonah had to be thrown overboard in order for the men and the ship to be saved. Do not hang around anyone running from the call of God because you will have to deal with their storm. God is merciful so He did not allow Jonah to drown. He created a great fish that swallowed him. Jonah prayed from the belly of the great fish and the Lord heard him and delivered. It is better to be in the storm because of obedience to God rather than disobedience.

The ship in which Paul traveled was hit with the typhoon because they failed to heed the warning he gave them. The crew had to let the ship drift because it was impossible to steer it. It is impossible to steer our lives so it is imperative that we allow the Captain of our salvation to do the steering. When the storm grew worse the sailors did everything they could to keep the hull of the boat from coming apart. They wrapped ropes or chains around the hull, they took down some of the sails and on the second day they started throwing some of the wheat overboard. On the third day they threw out the furnishings. When the midnight storm is raging in your life, it makes no sense to cling to things that will keep you heavy laden and cause your ship to sink. You can get new possessions but you cannot get another life. You can get another wife or another husband, but you cannot get another life. Job 1:4 says, "Skin for skin, yea, all that a man hath will he give for his life." What good are material possessions when you are going under? I have never seen a U Haul truck following the hearse in a funeral procession. Do not allow anyone to stress you out in the midnight hour because if you die from a stroke they will not get in the grave with you when your coffin is being lowered. The tempest caused so much darkness they could see neither the sun nor the stars so it was impossible to determine their position. Now that is what I call darkness.

Like Horatio Spafford there are many people that have lost loved ones. Unlike Mr. Spafford many of them have allowed the tragedy to cause them to question God and turn away from the faith. Some of them have souls that have become darkened by grief and sorrow, they do not know whether they are coming or going. I remember the afternoon in January when I received the call from my brother in-law informing me that my oldest brother was shot to death. His words reverberated through my soul. I had to fight depression and melancholy because I knew he was gone and he was not coming back. Throughout the whole process I kept remembering the word my pastor spoke to me when he said, "Shall not the God of the whole earth do right." In the midst of your darkest tragedy allow the light of the Lord Jesus to shine. Give no room to the devil by second guessing God.

Job's midnight came when he lost all of his children, sat in an ash heap scraping himself with a potsherd because his body had broken out with open sores from which pus oozed; his wife asked him if he still retained his integrity then told him to curse God and die. Job told her, *"Thou speakest as one of the foolish women speaketh. What? Shall we receive good at the hand of God, and shall we not receive evil? In all this did not Job sin with his lips" (Job 2:10).*

The ship on which Paul traveled was being tossed to and fro by the tempest Euroclydon but the man of God knew that he was destined for Rome so he had peace. God gives songs in the night and peace in the storm. Do not allow fear of death or any other type of fear to cripple you because you have a more sure word of prophecy, and a destination in God. God has spoken concerning where He is taking you and you must allow Him to lead you there. Do not take any detours. Stay in your lane and allow Him to drive and there will not be any wrecks. You might have some near misses but you will reach your destination. The Bible declares we should, *"Be careful for nothing; but in every thing by prayer and supplication with thanksgiving let your requests be made known unto God. And the peace of God, which passeth all understanding, shall keep your hearts and minds through Christ Jesus" (Philippians 4:6-7).* The Greek word for *keep* as it is used by Paul is phroureo (pronounced froo-reh-o). It has a military connotation. It means to be a watcher in advance, to mount guard as a sentinel, to post spies at gates, to hem in, to protect, and to keep with a garrison. Paul did not suffer panic or anxiety attacks because he had an active prayer life and gave God thanks continually. We must not allow any circumstance or situations, trials, or tribulations to cause us to become anxious. In everything we face we must pray, and give thanks. Never forget Paul and Silas, they prayed and before they received the answer they praised.

Paul backed up what he wrote to the churches with his actions. Remember, he is the one that declared to the Philippians, *"Not that I speak in respect of want: for I have learned, in whatsoever state I am, therewith to be content. I know both how to be abased, and I know how to abound: every where and in all things I am instructed both to be full and to be hungry, both abound and to suffer need. I can do all things through Christ which strengths me" (Philippians 4:11).* The strength of Christ makes the impossible possible; we have a tendency to trust in our own strength at times but we must resist that temptation. When Paul had the thorn in the flesh he prayed to God for its removal. He was informed by God that His mercy was sufficient and His strength would be perfected in Paul's weakness. When the Apostle found out God was perfecting strength through the weakness of the situation he said he would rather glory in his infirmities so the power of God could rest upon him. It is that type of posture and unwavering trust in God that kept him calm, cool, and collected in the tempest.

The situation on the ship seemed hopeless, and it stemmed from the unwillingness of the centurion Julius to listen the messenger of the Lord. My mother always told me, "if I made my bed hard I would have to lay in it, and "if I did not hear I would feel." I have been forced to sleep on many hard beds and felt a lot of pain because I refused to heed words of wisdom. Impatience and unwillingness can cause us to end up in tempestuous seas. Things were so dark that all hope of survival seemed to be lost. Paul gave a mild rebuke to the centurion and the master of the ship by telling them they should have listened to him. He went on to tell them to be of good cheer because no life would be lost. The only loss would be that of the ship.

I BELIEVE GOD

The Apostle had an angelic visitation and received a blessed assurance from the Lord. God had given Paul all the lives on the ship because he had to appear before Caesar. We serve a God of grace and mercy, a God of love and compassion. I love the fact the Apostle told them, *"Sirs, be of good cheer: for I believe God, that it shall be even as it was told me" (Acts 27:25).* God will not allow one of the promises spoken to us to be unfulfilled. He will honor His word and we have to trust Him to do so. When you take God at His word and stand on His promises you can have good cheer at midnight. My question to you the reader is this, **"DO YOU BELIEVE GOD?"**

When you are a servant of the Lord Jesus Christ you will always be in the majority when opposition comes against you. When Judas betrayed Jesus he came with a great multitude with swords and staves from the chief priests and elders of the people. One of Jesus' followers pulled a sword and cut off the ear of the servant of the high priests. *"Then said Jesus unto him, Put up again thy sword into his place: for all they that take the sword shall perish with the sword. Thinkest thou that I cannot now pray to my Father, and he shall presently give me more than twelve legions of angels" (Matthew 26:52-53)?* Twelve is the number of Divine government and apostolic fullness. As a believer you have angels assigned to you to war in the realm of the spirit for your breakthrough. Once of Paul's angels stood by him in the darkness of the night to assure him that all would be well.

When God is on your side you are not in the minority because you and God will be the majority in any battle. Paul understood this and that is why he did not waver when the centurion believed the master of the ship instead of believing him. Paul did not try to argue with them; he simply believed God. Our trust and confidence in God's word cannot waver, because the numbers are against us. The larger the giants the more glory God will receive. The key to the victory will be our willingness to believe by faith. Unbelief and a lack of faith are not pleasing to God. Jesus did not do many miracles in His own country because the people only saw Him as the carpenter's son, the Son of Mary, and the Brother of James, Joses, Simon, and Judas. There are many people that will not be able to receive from the anointing God has placed on our lives because of a spirit of familiarity and ignorance of who we are in Jesus.

The Bible says, *"But when the fourteenth night was come, as we were driven up and down in Adria, about midnight the shipmen deemed that they drew near to some country" (Acts 27:27)*. Fourteen is the number of Passover (Exodus 12:6; Numbers 9:5). Paul and the men who were with him were about to pass from death to life, because God had given His apostle assurance that he would go to Rome. No one desires to be in a life threatening storm. But, when you are in one make the best of it, because God can use it as an opportunity for you to witness and help others. Paul remained cool in the midst of the storm and his calmness and the fact that he had a word from the Lord at every juncture helped the men on the ship. It is good to have a man on the ship, who can pray, get a word from God, and have faith in that word as the storm gets worse, and people begin to panic.

What type of character traits are you displaying in the midst of your midnight situation? Are the people around you seeing the peace of God on you or do they see someone that is falling apart? How you handle the storms at midnight will have a positive or negative effect on the people around you. Out of your affliction the Lord will birth an anointing, out of your misery will come a great ministry, and out of the current mess God will give you a message for this messed age. Stand firm in your midnight trials because you are more than a conqueror; you are an over comer. Jesus' midnight came before He went to the cross. His midnight came in the Garden of Gethsemane where we saw the total surrendering of His will to His Father. When the winds start to blow and the rains come like a torrent; bow your head in prayer and let the Lord know you accept His will unconditionally.

I remember the first rough hurricane season in the city of Jacksonville Florida. Growing up in New York City meant freezing weather in the winter with a great deal of snow. I was very happy when I moved to Florida, but I did not realize how boisterous the wind can be during hurricane season. During one particularly rough season I looked out the window and saw oak trees bending in the wind as if they were about to be broken. The amazing thing is Jacksonville normally does not get hit as bad as other parts of Florida. When I heard the howling winds and saw branches flying around like they were paper I could not imagine the terror of a storm of a higher category. I can only imagine the sheer terror of being at sea for fourteen days, unable to see at certain points with the winds and the waves crashing against the ship until it felt like it was going to break. Paul was a great man of God in that he was like a Timex; He took a licking but kept on ticking. Living through one ship wreck was bad enough but three was incredible, and that's not counting the beatings and the stoning.

On the fourteenth day at midnight the crew took soundings and discovered that the water was getting shallower. From the roar of the waves they surmised that the ship was headed for the rocks. They were so afraid of hitting the rocks that some of the crew dropped four anchors while wishing for day. There is a time of darkness coming on this earth that will cause men to wish for some daylight. Jesus said, *"I must work the works of him that sent me, while it is day: the night cometh, when no man can work" (John 9:4).* The shipmen had no control of the boat because they were in darkness and the ship was being tossed by the storm. Some of the men decided it was time to escape by lowering the boat that was on the ship down into the sea.

When the midnight hour comes, some people will drop their anchors deeper in Jesus the solid rock while others will turn away from the faith. Paul told them no harm would come to them but midnight caused them to panic. Fear in the midnight hour will cause people to override good counsel; this is why we have to walk by faith and not by sight. There will be times in the life of the believer when a midnight crisis will cause our vision to be obscured; it is in these perilous times that we have to walk by the light of God's word. It will not be a cake walk because the adversary will come at us to make us doubt the word God has spoken to us. God's promises are yeah and amen but when the word does not come to pass fast enough in our lives it is easy to begin to doubt. The word of the Lord will be tested in our lives during the storm, but we must hold fast to the profession of our faith. Some of the men wanted to take matters into their own hands instead of trusting the word Paul gave. There was pandemonium and chaos on the ship because the shipmen were gripped with fear. Once again the man of God stood up and gave a word of exhortation.

The storms of life we go through will help us to help others in their time of trouble. When someone is going through a situation the Lord has already brought you through, you can encourage and strengthen them for the arduous journey. Paul had already been in multiple ship wrecks so he knew how to rest in the Lord while others were operating out of a spirit of fear. When tragedy strikes many people develop a mob mentality. God expects his servants to be a light in every dark situation. How can we help someone if we have never gone through anything ourselves?

The Apostle spoke boldly to the centurion Julius and said, "Except these abide in the ship, ye cannot be saved" (Acts 27:31). How ironic it is that Paul started out the journey as a prisoner but now he is the captain. Paul proves that one believer can bring a sense of calm to a midnight situation by standing on the word of Jesus and exercising faith in Him. Faith in Jesus can bring peace to a storm, light to a dark situation, and transform any atmosphere. The soldiers cut the rope to the boat that was tied to the ship so none of the men could escape. Once you anchor your soul in Jesus you must cut and sever ties to every worldly thing that will try to pull you away from Him. Once Paul told them to abide in the ship and they heeded his warning the day started to dawn and he encouraged them to take something to eat for their strength, because not one hair would fall from their head. Paul knew Jesus was in charge and He has counted every hair on our heads. If you are bald then he counts the follicles. After speaking to the men about eating, Paul took bread and gave thanks to God and ate it in their presence. When they saw Paul eating they took some bread and began to be cheerful.

We will have to fast in the midnight hour but the time will come when we will have to take meat in order to strengthen our bodies for the duration of the journey. People are watching to see our posture at the midnight hour; they are looking to see how we compose ourselves when everything is being shaken by the tempest of a Euroclydon typhoon. You must steady yourself in Jesus during the midnight hour, so others can know they too can have peace in the midst of the storm. The believer in Christ must not allow panic to set in and cause them to speak out of a spirit of doubt and fear because that is contagious and the people around will begin to panic. In the midnight tempest commit yourself to seeking the Lord for a word through fasting and prayer.

YOU CAN MAKE IT, EVEN ON BROKEN PIECES

We have to keep in mind that midnight is not only a time of the day but it is also a state or condition where all appears to be dark. Once it was daybreak the pilot of the ship decided to get the ship to shore. As the violent waves struck the ship the shipmen decided to pull up the anchors and head for a creek that had a shore hoping to thrust the ship in. They fell into a place where two seas met and ran the front of the ship aground, causing it to be unmovable. The hind part of the ship was destroyed by the violent waves. The body of Jesus was broken for us so we could receive eternal life. There were two hundred and seventy seven souls on the ship so they decided to lighten the ship by casting the wheat into the sea. Sea is symbolic of the restless masses of humanity, the wicked nations. (Isaiah 60:5; 57:20; James 1:6; Ezekiel 26: 3, 4). We do not need to be heavy laden and restless because of the cares of this life. Jesus said, *"Come unto me, all ye that labour and are heavy laden, and I will give you rest. Take my yoke upon you, and learn of me; for I am meek and lowly in heart: and ye shall find rest unto your souls. For my yoke is easy, and my burden is light" (Matthew 11:28-30).* Jesus is the burden bearer so if you are feeling heavy from the midnight experience, or the tempest that is tossing you around. Lighten your load by casting your cares upon Jesus for He cares for you

The soldiers took counsel to kill the prisoners so none of them would escape. A Roman soldier might have to forfeit his life if he lost a prisoner. "But the centurion, willing to save Paul, kept them from their purpose and commanded that they which could swim should cast themselves first into the sea and get to land" (Acts 27:43). The centurion that did not take Paul's word at the beginning of the journey knew that Paul should be protected. He had seen time and again how the word of the Lord came through Paul and saved their lives. This is the reason why we cannot afford any fleshly outbursts when the midnight hour is upon us. The same people who doubt us will have to admit the Lord is speaking in and through us. God had pre-determined that His Apostle should preach the gospel at Rome and he would protect the life of everyone on the ship just to do it. Beloved God has a plan for your life and if you can trust Him in the rough stormy midnight season, He will deliver you and give you souls.

Some of the men on the ship were able to get to land because they knew how to swim, but concerning the rest the Bible says, "And the rest, some on boards, and some on the broken pieces of the ship, And so it came to pass, that they escaped all safe to land" (Acts 27:44). Beloved, you can make it to land even if you have to cling to the altar, to the pew, or one of the pillars in the church. The important thing is that you make it. It does not matter if you make it by clinging to a fragment of something that is broken. The thing you must settle in your spirit is that the body of the Lord Jesus was bruised, so cling to Him in the midst of the storm and He will get you to land. Our journey into the Kingdom of God will take us through some midnight seasons but keep holding on to Jesus because He paid for your ticket with a bruised and beaten body. Your ticket was paid for by His precious blood that flowed from every stripe that He took for you. Do not be depressed by the fact that your life seems to be broken and fragmented because Jesus told His disciples to "gather up the fragments so nothing would be lost." God is going to get glory even out of the fragmented broken areas of your life. Your brokenness is the thing that will help people who cannot swim get to land.

FIND CHRIST IN THE CRISIS

There is a fascinating story in the Bible of three individuals who needed Jesus to intervene in a crisis situation; each individual exercised a different level of faith and each received the blessing they needed. The first person was Jairus and he was the ruler of the synagogue. He fell at the feet of Jesus and asked Him to come into his house. Jairus' 12 year old daughter was sick and was dying. She was an only child which probably made the situation more desperate. While Jesus was on the way to Jairus' house He was thronged by a multitude. One of the people in the group was a woman with an issue of blood; she had a serious midnight crisis that needed immediate attention like Jairus. She had the issue of blood for twelve years; notice the fact the number of divine government and apostolic fullness is mentioned twice. Two is the number of witness, testimony, and separation. Jesus came in apostolic and divine authority. His power over death and the grave gave witness to that fact.

The woman with the issue of blood had spent all her resources going to physicians and none of them could heal her. If you have ever had a long term illness you know how expensive it is to get proper medical care. You can spend yourself into poverty and still not be healed. The woman came behind Jesus in the crowd and touched the border of His garment and immediately her issue of blood dried. Jesus felt the virtue go out of Him and asked, *"Who touched me" (Luke 8:45)*. The Greek word for *virtue* as it is used here is *dunamis* and it means force, especially miraculous power, ability, might. When the woman came trembling before Jesus and explained to Him why she touched Him, Jesus told her to go in peace because her faith had made her whole. There is a type of faith that activates and unlocks the door to the miraculous. I always hear preachers of the word quote a portion of Ephesians 3:20, "Now unto him that is able to do exceeding abundantly above all that we ask or think." However, many of them never quote the last part that says, "according to the power that worketh in us." The Greek word for power used here is the same Greek word Jesus used for virtue when He told the people He felt the virtue go out of Him. The word is *dunamis*. Our ability to experience the exceeding, the abundant, and the above will be determined by our willingness to detonate the dynamite that is in us. Faith is the key to unleashing the dunamis power inside of us. The woman with the issue of blood had it and she fought through the crowds to pull the dunamis out of Jesus that she needed for her miracle.

The amazing thing about the woman with the issue of blood is this, according to the Levitical laws she should not have been in the midst of the people because of her issue. Leviticus 15:19, 25 states, "And if a woman has an issue, and her issue in her flesh be blood, she shall be put apart seven days: and whosoever toucheth her shall be unclean until the even. And if a woman have an issue of her blood many days out of the time of her separation, or if it run beyond the time of her separation; all the days of the issue of her uncleanness shall be as the days of her separation: she shall be unclean." This woman was well beyond the seven days mentioned in Leviticus 15. She bled for 12 long years. Please do not miss this revelation. She did not break the law when she sought to touch Jesus because He was the fulfillment and the embodiment of the law. Paul said, *"For Christ is the end of the law for righteousness to everyone that believeth" (Romans 10:4).* The purpose of the law was to teach the Israelites how to live holy before God. When the law was broken the blood of an innocent animal had to be shed. In Jesus she was seeing the Lamb of God that would be slain for her sins. Jesus said, *"Think not that I am come to destroy the law, or the prophets: I am not come to destroy, but to fulfill" (Matthew 5:17).* The religion of legalism will attempt to hold us back from Jesus by pointing out our issues, but grace will take us to a place in God where legalism cannot, that place is the feet of Jesus.

While Jesus was speaking to the woman someone form Jairus' house came and told Jairus not to trouble Jesus because his daughter was dead. It is never a bother to Jesus when there is a need. Jairus might have thought that if Jesus had accompanied him immediately his daughter would still be alive, but Jesus had power over death and the grave. Anytime He showed up would be the right time. When Jesus heard the report His response was, *"Fear not: believe only, and she shall be made whole" (Luke 8:50).* Fear and Faith are diametrically opposed to each other like light and darkness; where one is the other will not be. The first thing Jesus had to do was to deal with the spirit of fear that was coming on Jairus because of the report he received. When Jesus arrived at the house the only ones allowed in with Him were Peter, James, John, and the parents. The three disciples are the ones who went on the Mount of Transfiguration with Jesus.

There was weeping and wailing at Jairus' house so Jesus told the mourners not to weep because the child was sleeping and not dead. "And they laughed him to scorn, knowing that she was dead" (Luke 8:53). What dishonor and disrespect to Jesus; but I love His response. Jesus put all the doubters and the mockers out. Anyone who comes with a word that is contrary to what Jesus says you have to put them out. Jesus took her by the hand and said, "Maid arise." At the command of Jesus her spirit came back into her and she arose immediately. "After that miracle Jesus called His twelve disciples together, and gave them power and authority over all devils, and to cure diseases. And He sent them to preach the kingdom of God and to heal the sick"

The third story involved a centurion who needed Jesus to heal his servant who was sick with palsy and grievously tormented. Jesus agreed to go and heal his servant. The centurion told Jesus he was unworthy to have Him under his roof. He said Jesus should speak the word only and his servant would be healed. *Psalm 107:20 declares, "He sent his word, and healed them, and delivered them from their destructions."* Jairus' faith required Jesus to go into his house, the woman with the issue of blood had the type of faith that said, "If I touch the border of His garment I will be made whole, and the centurion's faith said, "speak the word only." The centurion understood the chain of command because he was under authority and he had soldiers under his authority. He knew how to follow authority and have the people under him follow authority. Jesus marveled at the words of the centurion and told His followers, "I have not found so great faith, no, not in Israel. What an awesome compliment given to the Gentile centurion. Jesus told the centurion to go his way because his belief had given him what he needed. His servant was healed the same hour. Contrast the attitude of the centurion towards Jesus and the attitude of the centurion who was taking Paul to Rome. The centurion who needed healing for his servant knew the power of the word that came from Jesus. The centurion who took Paul doubted the word of the Lord that came from Paul. The servant of the centurion received life from Jesus' words while the centurion who doubted almost lost his life in the storm.

No matter how difficult your journey, no matter how boisterous the storm, no matter how difficult the test, continue to believe God.

Your faith is one of your best assets so utilize it when the odds are against you. *In Romans 1:17 Paul quotes Habakkuk 2:4 when he said, "The Just shall live by faith."* Living by faith does not mean we are merely eking out an existence. It means we have an expectation of overcoming all obstacles and walking in overflow. We must trust God's perfect will for our lives because He will never leave us or forsake us. He will be with you in the storm. There are people whose lives are spared because they are associated with you and God has a plan for your life. The centurion and the men on the ship found out that Paul was a man of God.

HIDE ME IN THE CLEFT OF THE ROCK

There is a hiding place, a secret place in God that He uses to shelter us in times of tempestuous storms. He did not say we would not have to endure some storms, but as we go through there is a resting place for our minds. "He that dwelleth in the secret place of the most High shall abide under the shadow of the Almighty. I will say of the LORD, He is my refuge and my fortress: my God; in him will I trust" (Psalm 91:1-2). The Psalmist tells us not to be afraid for the terror by night; nor for the arrow that flieth by day. Paul and the men who were on the ship had to deal with the uncertainty of the dark night, and when daybreak came the ship was being struck violently by waves. But, in the midst of the storm Paul was able to say, "I believe God." God is no respecter of persons; Paul knew He belonged to God and in your midnight hour you must rest in the secret place your Father has provided. The LORD told Moses that he could not see His face and live, but there was a place by Him where Moses could stand upon a rock and when His glory passed by He would put Moses in the cleft of the rock, and would cover him with His hand as he passed by (Exodus 33:20-22). Beloved the rock upon which we are to stand to see the glory of God is none other than the Lord Jesus Christ. The songwriter wrote, "On Jesus the solid rock I stand, all other ground is sinking sand." There is a place by our heavenly Father and Jesus was wounded to get us into that place. When the storms of life are raging, when the darkness becomes unbearable, just worship your way into that place by Him for He will protect you and give you peace.

THE SECRET PLACE

When Saul tried to kill David his son Jonathan told David to abide in a secret place, and hide himself. You can find the secret place in worship. Worship is the key to entering in. You must praise God for the things He has done but you must worship Him for who He is. Job asked the LORD to keep him secret, until His wrath passed; He asked Him to appoint him a set time, and remember him. Then Job asked the question, *"If a man die, shall he live again? all the days of my appointed time will I wait, till my change come" (Job 14:14).* Every man who dies will live again it is just a matter of where that man will live again. They who have their lives hid in the secret place of God in Christ Jesus will find eternal rest in Him and those who do not enter His rest will live in darkness.

The psalmist David said, *"For in the time of trouble he shall hide me in his pavilion: in the secret of his tabernacle shall he hide me; he shall set me upon a rock. And now shall mine head be lifted up above mine enemies round about me: therefore will I offer in his tabernacle sacrifices of joy; I will sing, yea, I will sing praises unto the LORD" (Psalm 27:5).* When David was surrounded by his enemies he did not fear because he knew there was a secret place in God where he would be protected. Fear, worry, and doubt are some of the tools the devil uses to keep us out of the secret place. He knows if we can find a place in worship during the storm we will have peace. I cannot impress on you enough the importance of resting in God in your night seasons. Please meditate on these psalms and use them when the winds and the waves begin to beat your ship. David said, *"Thou shalt hide them in the secret of thy presence from the pride of man: thou shalt keep them secretly in a pavilion from the strife of tongues" (Psalm 31:20).* Do not be deterred by the criticisms of the tongues of men that have come against you. You do not have to justify yourself when there is a verbal attack against your character. When your name has been slandered and dragged through the mud by church people, when you have been the victim of character assassination God will hide you in the secret place of His pavilion. Who can penetrate that secret place in God and pull you out? In the Song of Songs king Solomon wrote, *"O my dove, that art in the clefts of the rock, in the secret places of the stairs, let me see thy countenance, let me hear thy voice; for sweet is thy voice, and thy countenance is comely" (SS 2:14).*

GIANT KILLER

David understood the importance of worship and that is why he was called a man after God's heart. He knew there was a place in God that the enemy could not penetrate, no matter how big or strong they were. He knew giants could not stand in defiance of the people of God because God towered over all giants. His encounter with the giant Goliath of Gath is an example to us why we should not fear the giant situations that come at us in the midnight hour. When the Israelites were facing the prospect of battling Goliath they were terrified because of his height and stature. When David found out what was going on he wanted to know, "Who is this uncircumcised Philistine, that he should defy the armies of the living God" (1 Samuel 17:26b). David understood that Goliath had no covenant and therefore he could not stand in battle. When God cut the covenant with Abraham He signified that Abraham's enemies were His enemies. This held true for the descendants of Abraham of which we are included because we have been engrafted into the covenant by the blood of Jesus. When He cut the covenant with Abraham blood had to be shed. In order to bring us into the covenant blessings, the blood of Jesus had to be shed. In the days of Abraham the adopted son had the same rights and privileges as the son born in the house. When we face giants we must remember the covenant that we have with God.

David was a young man when Goliath came against the people of Israel but he was an experienced young man. He witnessed God deliver his father's lamb from the mouth of the lion and the bear; He expected God to do the same with Goliath. Goliath drew near to the armies of Israel morning and evening and presented himself forty days. The evening always comes before the morning. Light has to be called out of darkness. Goliath tormented the armies of Israel morning and evening for forty days. The number forty is symbolic of testing and probation. David was delivering lunches to his brothers on the battlefield when he heard the giant disrespecting Israel's army. When the soldiers of Israel saw the giant they were so afraid that they fled. Young David had to tell King Saul not to let the heart of the men fail because he would go and fight the Philistine. Goliath was a battle tested warrior and David was a youth, but David had something the Giant did not have and that was a covenant with the Almighty God.

God does not change because we face a different enemy; He can handle lions, bears, and Philistine giants. When Saul offered to give David his armour he refused them because he had not proved them. The Hebrew word for prove is nacah (pronounced naw-saw) and it means to test, try, and to destroy. When we face giants we have to know our weapons. We have to utilize the ones previously proven in battle. We have proven ourselves with prayer and worship and these are the weapons we must use. David's weapon of choice was a sling and a smooth stone, and that is what he drew near to the Philistine with. The Philistine was shocked when he saw David; he could not believe that Israel had sent a youth out against a seasoned soldier like him. When the enemy looks at us he is going to be surprised. Though we look young and inexperienced against his seasoned demons, we are coming in the name of the Lord of hosts and that is what makes the difference. Goliath disdained David because he was young and looked like he could not kill an ant. When the giant threatened to feed David's flesh to the fowls of the air, and to the beasts of the field, David responded by saying, "Thou comest to me with a sword, and with a spear, and with a shield: but I come to thee in the name of the LORD of hosts, the God of the armies of Israel whom thou hast defied" David promised that on that day the LORD would deliver Goliath into his hand and he would cut off his head and give his body to the fowls of the air, and to the wild beasts of the earth so all the earth would know that there is a God in Israel.

The Lord Jesus has given us weapons and the armour we need for battle. If we stick to the weapons He has given us we are assured victory. We get into trouble when we go against the giants with man made weapons. Paul said, "For the weapons of our warfare are not carnal, but mighty through God to the pulling down of strongholds; casting down imaginations, and every high thing that exalteth itself against the knowledge of God, and bringing into captivity every thought to the obedience of Christ" (2 Corinthians 10:4).

David's main contention with the Philistine was his defiance of the people of God. David knew that by defying God's people Goliath was defying God and he was not about to let that happen because he had a love and a zeal for God. Goliath despised him so much that he cursed him by his gods. He had a bunch of gods, but David had the Almighty God. David gave God the glory by telling Goliath that "the LORD saveth not with sword and spear: for the battle is the LORD's." Never go against a giant in your own strength; go with the understanding that the battle is not ours. It is God's because He fights our battles.

There is a spiritual principle behind the Philistine Giant. He is a type of the enemy that attacks the people of God day and night. The giant for us may be a stronghold in the mind that is trying to exalt itself against the knowledge of God. The Lord has given us the weapons needed to bring down the stronghold. David utilized his weapon effectively when he ran towards Goliath and sunk the stone in his forehead causing him to fall on his face. We should not run from giants, we should run to them with the rock. David had a stone but we have a rock and He is solid.

David battled a literal giant in Goliath but we have to battle spiritual giants that manifest themselves in things like sickness, disease, and infirmities just to name a few. Paul said, "For we wrestle not against flesh and blood, but against principalities, against, powers, against the rulers of the darkness of this world, against spiritual wickedness in high places" (Ephesians 6:12). We are not in a long distance war against the forces of darkness; we are in a wrestling match. It is important to understand that our enemies are not people but it is the principalities and the powers that are operating behind the scenes.

Paul went on to tell the Ephesians to put on the whole armor of God so they would be able to withstand in the evil day. The believer's armor is Truth, Righteousness, The preparation of the gospel of peace, The shield of faith, The helmet of salvation, and The sword of the Spirit, which is the word of God. Paul lists the final weapon as praying in the Spirit. Why in the Spirit? Because the Spirit makes intercession for us since He knows the mind of Christ.

On page 237 of his book, The Basics, author Gene Cunningham wrote, "In Ephesians 6:11, Paul tells us to put on the full armor of God, that we may be able to stand firm against the "schemes" of the devil. Here the word is methodeia, which means "cunning arts, deceit, craft, trickery." We have to remember that our enemy is not only a master strategist; he is also a cheat and a liar. In the Ephesians passage Paul goes on to say that "our struggle is not against flesh and blood" but against the spiritual forces of wickedness. The word translated "struggle" is pale, a term for "hand-to hand combat."

David was able to cut the head of the giant off with his own sword. We will cut the head of the giants that have come against us with our sword which is the word of God. The word of God in the hand of the believer is two edged, it cuts going in and it cuts going out. All the Philistines fled when their champion Goliath was dead.

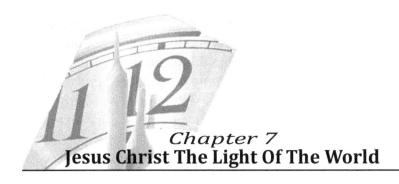

Chapter 7
Jesus Christ The Light Of The World

The only way to get rid of darkness is to turn on the light. The greater the level of darkness the more light we have to shine. Since midnight represents the darkest points of our journey in God, the Lord Jesus is the only solution to the demonic attacks we face at midnight. He has provided the tools or what I call the floodlights that will help us to navigate in the night. Prayer, fasting, praise, and worship are essential tools, and so is His word. The Psalmist David declared, *"The entrance of thy words giveth light; it giveth understanding unto the simple" (Psalm 119:130).* The Hebrew word for simple is pethiy (pronounced peh-thee); it means *silly, seducible, foolish.* When the word of God enters our lives and we act on the word, it moves us from foolishness to wisdom, from darkness to light. Light dispels darkness, so the believer can make forward progress. The more of His word we walk in, the better equipped we are to resist seducing spirits. *"Wherewithal shall a young man cleanse his way? By taking heed thereto according to they word" (Psalm 119:9).* We tend to take a great deal of risk when we are young, and we are more susceptible to the tricks of the devil. The light of the gospel will cleanse the way of young immature men.

When I speak of light I am not speaking exclusively of the light emanating from the sun, the moon, the stars or the light that shines when the light switch is turned on. I am also referring to information from the word of God which dispels the darkness of ignorance so the believer's steps can be ordered. Jesus said, *"The light of the body is the eye: if therefore thine eye be single, thy whole body shall be full of light. But if thine eye be evil, thy whole body shall be full of darkness.*

If therefore the light that is in thee be darkness, how great is that darkness" (Matthew 6:22-23)! Jesus is telling us we should keep our eyes focused on Him and not on the things of this world.

David declared, *"Thy word is a lamp unto my feet, and a light unto my path" (Psalm 119:105).* Our feet speak of our walk with the Lord and the only way we can complete our journey is by walking in the light of His word. *"Where there is no vision, the people perish: but he that keepeth the law, happy is he" (Proverbs 29:18).* The Hebrew word for vision as it is used here is chazown (pronounced khaw-zone) and it means to see *mentally*, a *dream*, a *revelation* or an *oracle*. Vision is more than the ability to see optically.

The writer is saying, without a revelation or an oracle the people will perish because it is impossible to survive without light. Without the sun, humans, plants, and animals would perish. In the same manner, all would perish without the light that emanates from the word of the Son. Through a process called photosynthesis, plants and animals receive energy from the light of the sun; without this light, life could not be sustained on the earth. The Hebrew word for perish is *para* and it means to expose, dismiss, to uncover or be naked. When there is no oracle or revelation from God, the people are exposed and uncovered by the adversary.

When you study Ezekiel 37 you will see an open valley full of dry bones. The bones were a picture of a nation that was perishing because they refused to heed the word of God. The bones were able to come alive because Ezekiel prophesied as the LORD commanded him. God instructed Ezekiel to, *"Prophesy unto these bones, and say unto them, O ye dry bones, hear the word of the LORD. Thus saith the Lord God unto these bones; Behold, I will cause breath to enter into you, and y shall live. (Ezekiel 37 4-5).* Ezekiel declared, "So I prophesied as I was commanded: and as I prophesied, there was a noise, and behold a shaking, and the bones came together, bone to his bone" (Ezekiel 37:7). The bones came together in the right order. The word of God brings life, order and it brings structure. The word of God is synonymous with light and ignorance of the word of God is synonymous with darkness and confusion. *Job 33:4* declares, *"The Spirit of God hath made me, and the breath of the Almighty hath given me life."* This is the reason the Apostle Paul declared that, *"All scripture is given by inspiration of God, and is profitable for doctrine, for reproof, for correction, for instruction in righteousness: That the man of God may be perfect, thoroughly furnished unto all good works"* *(2 Timothy 3:16).* It is impossible for any individual to come to a place of maturity, completion, or perfection without the scriptures. The Greek word translated "inspired by God" is theopneustos, from Theos, God, and pneuma, breath. Paul is saying, "All scripture is God breathed." It is imperative that we understand the importance of God's word to our spirits, souls, and our bodies. The word of God to the believer is what the breath is to the human body. God's word is alive and He breathed it into Adam when He created Him. *"And the LORD God formed man of the dust of the ground, and breathed into his nostrils the breath of life; and man became a living soul" (Genesis 2:7).* The fall of Adam was caused by his disobedience of God's word, and his fall brought death into the world. Jesus Christ is called the last Adam because He is the perfect expression of God's word, and He has come to restore us to life.

We have to set time aside on a daily basis to search out the principles and the keys hidden in the scriptures. There is a scripture that will help us in every dark situation we face. When you study the scriptures you see men and women who had a love and a passion for the word of God. They meditated and applied His word to their lives and were able to overcome the obstacles that tried to hinder their walk with God. We live in a time where things appear to be moving at a very fast pace. If we are not careful, the cares of this life will cause us to neglect the meditation and the application of the word of God. When we neglect His word we will miss the principles He has embedded in the word for our direction and growth. It is impossible for us to apply something we do not have. If a house has not been wired for light then light can not be turned on when it is dark. Only what is inside an individual can come out, and for this reason the onus is on every believer to spend quality time reading and studying the word of God.

HE'S AN ONTIME GOD

Self publishing is a costly endeavor. When I finished the manuscript for my second book, Perceive and Receive, I needed finances to get it edited, formatted, and to get the cover designed. I stood on my faith in God and His promise to supply all of my needs according to His riches in glory by Christ Jesus. I set the date for my book release, but I did not get the manuscript and the cover to the company that was going to print the books. I went to a local printer to see if he could print enough for me to have for the book signing. He told me the amount I needed would cost one thousand dollars. It was on a Saturday, and I told him I would return on Monday. I did not have the money, but, **I believed God.** I was slated to speak at church on Sunday, and the message the Lord gave me was based on Hebrews 11 and Romans 10:8. It was a message on living faith. When I finished preaching a lady walked over to me and handed me a check. I put it in my pocket while I conversed with some of the people. Not long thereafter I took a look at the check and it was for one thousand dollars. The exact amount quoted to me by the gentleman at the local printing company. God is an on time God, He may not come when you want Him, but He will always be on time. God knows exactly what we need when we need it.

The next Sunday I went to the lady and told her how I needed one thousand dollars for the printing of my book. She broke into tears when I told her that. She said God spoke to her that morning and told her to write me a check. When she asked the Lord how much, He told her He would show her when she arrived at church. While I was speaking on faith, God was sending an H-mail to her. Email is electronic mail but an H-mail is a heavenly or Holy Ghost mail. I did not mention a thing about needing a thousand dollars while I was preaching. God by His sovereign and supernatural power spoke to that precious sister and told her the exact amount I needed. She was in a place spiritually where she could hear God speak to her, and she was mature enough to obey. God knows exactly the amount you need right now, and He is downloading an H mail to someone to give it to you. Hallelujah!!! Stand on His promise, *"For all the promises of God in Jesus Christ are yea, and in him Amen, unto the glory of God by us"* (2 Corinthians 1:20).

Here is a scripture to hammer home the point of the importance of standing in faith in the midnight hour. *"But without faith it is impossible to please him: for he that cometh to God must believe that he is, and that he is a rewarder to them that diligently seek him" (Hebrews 11:6).* Without the kind of faith that motivates us to trust in God, it would be impossible to please Him. Notice, the reward does not go to the believer, it goes to the diligent. The Apostle James said, *"Thou believest that there is one God; thou doest well: the devils also believe, and tremble" (James 2:19).*

Belief in one God is not a means in itself but a means to an end. It is the first step on a life long journey. The reward is the "the prize of the high calling of God in Christ Jesus." Belief gets a person salvation and protects him from the judgment and the wrath that is to come. Remember Paul said, *"That if thou confess with thy mouth the Lord Jesus, and shalt believe in thine heart that God hath raised him from the dead, thou shalt be saved" (Romans 10:9).* So, belief in the one true God secures salvation, but the reward goes to the believers who are willing to act on their belief. The reward goes to the diligent. Diligently in Greek is ekzeteo, and it means, to search out, crave, demand, worship, to seek after carefully. It is easy to talk about faith when the light is shining and the blessings are flowing.

The diligent are the believers who have a living, active, vibrant faith that motivates them to work the work of the Lord. The word seek in Hebrews 11:6 is the same Greek word found in Matthew 6:33. It is the word zeteo, which means to worship God. God is brining a people through the wilderness, through the furnace of affliction and through various midnight seasons, a people who are hungering and thirsting after His righteousness. A people like the woman of Canaan who needed a healing for her daughter. She found Jesus when He hid in a house and would have no man know it. The Bible declares, "But he could not be hidden." He could not be hidden, because there was a woman seeking Him who understood the ekzeteo principle. She craved, and demanded an audience with Him, and she would not be denied. His word tells us we can come before the throne boldly to obtain mercy in the time of our need. He does not want us to limp or to come into His presence with fear and trepidation; He wants us to come boldly. The darker the hour, the bolder our approach should be. There is enough mercy at His throne to help with any need, no matter how great.

Midnight is a principle in the scriptures. When we understand the principle of midnight and the Biblical keys to overcome it, we will walk in the favor and the victory of God. Midnight represents the time of great need, but God's mercy is waiting to be poured out to meet the need. To fully comprehend and appreciate light, we have to experience darkness. Midnight gives us a greater appreciation for the light.

GROSS DARKNESS

The prophet Isaiah is called the eagle eyed prophet because he had a God given ability to see far into the future. He told the nation of Israel to, *"Arise, shine; for thy light is come, and the glory of the LORD is risen upon thee" (Isaiah 60:1).* He was encouraging the nation by letting them know that God was going to redeem them, and then he would use them to be a light to the nations. They were to reveal God's word and glory to the nations of the earth. He went on to tell them that, *"darkness shall cover the earth, and gross darkness the people: but the LORD shall arise upon them, and his glory shall be seen upon them."* When God saves an individual, He has a greater purpose than just taking that individual to heaven. God saves us so we can be vessels carrying His word and His glory.

When believers are living according to the word of God, people in darkness will see the light of God emanating from them. The problem today is many people are seeing flesh covered over by religious activities and they know that it is not the true light. Jesus declared, *"Woe unto you scribes and Pharisees, hypocrites! For ye are like unto whited sepulchers, which indeed appear beautiful outward, but are within full of dead men's bones, and of all uncleanness" (Matthew 23:27).* The Pharisees were experts in the laws of God given to Moses for His people. They were supposed to teach the people, but instead they perverted the Law of God and used it to keep the people in bondage. We were given the word of God so our lives and the lives of others could be transformed. Search the scriptures and you will see individuals God called and used to impact nations, by bringing His word to them.

God had a Divine purpose for calling Abram out of the land of Ur of the Chaldees. Ur was one of the oldest and most famous of the Babylonian cities. The people of Ur were moon worshipers. In the book of Revelation the Apostle John describes the false religious system when he declared, *"And upon her forehead was a name written, MYSTERY, BABYLON THE GREAT, THE MOTHER OF HARLOTS AND ABOMINATIONS OF THE EARTH" (Revelation 17:5).* It is a false religious system that seduces people with a pseudo light. In the same manner in which the Almighty God called Abram out of the abomination of moon worship, He is calling a people out of the seduction of modern Babylonian pseudo worship.

The people of Ur were looking to be enlightened by worshipping the moon but the moon only reflects the light of the sun. It is not wise to worship something which gets its light from another source. Why worship the reflection when you can worship the Son of righteousness. There may be some validity to astrology in terms of the alignment of the stars and their ability to give direction in certain instances, but it is an abomination for people to put their trust in that system. Why look to the stars for direction when you can go directly to Jesus Christ, the star maker? When the wise men sought Jesus they declared, *"Where is he that is born King of the Jews? For we have seen his star in the east, and are come to worship him" (Matthew 2:2).* Wise men are the ones who seek Jesus. They followed the lesser light to get to the greater light. *"And God made two great lights; the greater light to rule the day, and the lesser light to rule the night" he made the stars also. And God set them in the firmament of the heaven to give light upon the earth, And to rule over the day and over the night, and to divide the light from the darkness: from the darkness: and God saw that it was good" (Genesis 1:16-18).* Every believer God has brought out of darkness into His marvelous light is set in the earth to radiate the light of Jesus Christ. The patriarch Abraham was the person used by God to get the process started.

God had a plan for Abram's life so he called him from his country, from his kindred, and from his father's house. He promised him blessings if he would be obedient. The Hebrew word for kindred is *mowledeth,* and it means birth place, lineage, offspring, or family. It comes from the word *yalad,* which means, to bear young; to beget; to act as midwife; specifically, to show lineage. Out of the loins of Abraham, a nation would be born, and out of that nation would come Jesus Christ the Messiah, the Light of the world. In-order for that to take place, Abram would have to leave all that was familiar to him to embrace the promise of God. You and I must be willing to forsake all if necessary, in order for God to birth His purpose through us.

God had a Divine purpose when He changed the name from Abram, which means exalted father, to Abraham which means father of a multitude. The amazing thing about the promise is, Abram was ninety-nine years old, and his wife Sarah was ninety and barren. God's purpose and plans for our lives will not be hindered by age or barrenness. God had a Divine purpose when he called Abraham's descendants out of slavery in Egypt. God's plan was to prepare a people and bring the nations one step closer to receiving the Messiah. Isaiah sums it up in verse 3 of chapter 60 by saying, *"And the Gentiles shall come to thy light, and kings to the brightness of thy rising."* The only way the gentiles will be able to come is when they are drawn to the marvelous light of Jesus Christ. From searching the scriptures we get an understanding that the world will be engrossed in gross darkness before the return of Jesus.

The prophet Jeremiah told the people they should give glory to God before he caused darkness, and before their feet stumbled upon the dark mountains. If they did not give God glory, the light they sought would be turned into the shadow of death and be made gross darkness (Jeremiah 13:16). When people look to other sources of light than Jesus Christ they are seduced into false doctrine and do not realize they are in darkness.

In *Matthew 13* Jesus spoke about a people whose ears have waxed gross, a people whose ears were dull of hearing, and whose eyes were closed so they could not see, hear nor understand. When motives are not pure people will not be able to properly discern the truths that are found in the scriptures. When we examine the state of the world today, we must concur that the prophetic words concerning darkness and gross darkness are coming to pass expeditiously. It is time for the children of God to arise and shine so unbelievers can see the light of the glorious gospel of Jesus Christ.

JESUS CHRIST IS THE LIGHT OF THE WORLD

The Apostle John declared, *"In the beginning was the Word, and the Word was with God, and the Word was God" (John 1:1).* John does not tell us when the beginning was, but he does tell us that God the Father was there and so was God the Word. The Greek word for Word is logos and it does not only mean something spoken; it means a *thought, reasoning,* or the *Divine expression.* Jesus Christ is the bodily manifestation of the Divine thought. In his letter to the Colossian church, Paul wrote, *"For in him dwelleth all the fullness of the Godhead bodily" (Colossians 2:9).* When we understand the revelation found at the beginning of John's gospel, it will dispel any and every false doctrine concerning the Deity of the Lord Jesus Christ. There was no point in the beginning when Jesus Christ was created as some teach because John said, *"all things were made by Him and without Him was not any thing made."*

Genesis 1 gives us the record of creation and John 1 gives us the record of the Pre-incarnate Christ who created all things. In his letter to the Colossians the apostle Paul went on to say, "For by him were all things created, that are in heaven, and that are in earth, visible and invisible, whether they be thrones, or dominions, or principalities, or powers: all things were created by him, and for him: And he is before all things, and by him all things consist. The Jehovah's Witnesses love to take Paul's words out of context when he said Christ is "the firstborn of every creature." In no way, shape, or form is Paul saying Christ was created. John declared, *"All things were made by Him."* Only God can create and surely it is absurd to think that Jesus created Himself.

On page 132 of his book titled *Baker Encyclopedia of Christian Apologetics*, Dr. Norman L. Geisler wrote, *"Jehovah's Witnesses use John 1:1 to show that Jesus was "a god," not, "the God," because no definite article appears in the Greek. This misunderstands both the language and the verse. In Greek, the definite article is normally used to stress "the individual, and when it is not present the reference is to "the nature" of the one denoted. Thus, the verse can be rendered, "And the Word was of the nature of God." In the context of the following verses and the rest of John (for example, 1:3; 8:5; 10:30; 20:28) it is impossible that John 1:1 suggests that Jesus is anything less than divine. The rest of the New Testament joins John in forthrightly proclaiming that Jesus is God (for example, in Colossians 1:15-16 and Titus 2:13)."* Dr. Geisler went on to say, *"Critics also use Colossians 1:15, where Paul classifies Christ as "firstborn of all creation." This seems to imply that Christ is a creature, the first creature as the universe was made. This interpretation likewise is contrary to the context, for Paul in Colossians 1:16 has just said that Christ "created all things" and he is about to say that "the fullness of the Godhead" is in him (2:9). The term firstborn frequently refers to a position of preeminence in the family which it clearly does in this context (cf. 1:18). Christ is heir of all things, creator and owner. He is before all things.* The Deity of the Lord Jesus Christ is central to the Bible, and there are a plethora of scriptures that confirms His Deity. *"Jesus claimed to be Yahweh when He prayed, "And now, O Father, glorify thou me with thine own self with the glory which I had with thee before the world was" (John 17:5). But Yahweh of the Old Testament said, "my glory will I not give to another" (Isaiah 42:8). Jesus also declared, "I am the first and the last" (Revelation 1:17). These are precisely the words used by Jehovah in Isaiah 42:8. He said, "I am the good shepherd" (John 10:11). But the Old Testament said, "Yahweh is my shepherd" (Psalm 23:1)."*

The Scriptures must be interpreted line upon line and precept upon precept to gain a clearer understanding; please allow me give you another line from the scriptures. Paul told Timothy, *"And without controversy great is the* mystery *of godliness: God was manifested in the flesh, justified in the Spirit, seen of angels, preached unto the Gentiles, believed on in the world, received up into glory" (1 Timothy 3:16).* The Greek word Paul used for mystery *is musterion.* It is from a derivative of the word *muo* which means to shut the mouth; a secret or "mystery" through the idea of silence imposed by initiation into religious rites.

Godliness and the Deity of Jesus Christ is a mystery to those who have not surrendered their hearts to Him, and confessed Him as both Lord and Savior. There is no controversy for the disciple to whom Jesus Christ has revealed Himself. Religion will always bind people with false doctrine but to the children of God the mystery has been revealed. When it was revealed, the darkness of ignorance concerning the Son of God dissipated and gave way to the light of the knowledge of Him. The Prophet Isaiah declared, *"For unto us a child is born, unto us a son is given: And the government shall be upon his shoulder: And his name shall be called Wonderful, Counsellor, The mighty God, The everlasting Father, The Prince of Peace. (Isaiah 9:6).* Who was that child that son? It is the same son whose parents found Him in the temple, sitting in the midst of the doctors, both hearing them, and asking them questions. And all that heard him were astonished at his understanding and answers" (Luke 2: 46-47). I do not believe He was asking them questions because He needed some knowledge they had. I believe He was asking them the type of questions which provoke thought. It is the same child Peter spoke of when he said, *"The kings of the earth stood up, and the rulers were gathered together against the Lord against his Christ. For of a truth against the holy child Jesus, who thou hast anointed, both Herod, and Pontius Pilate, with the Gentiles, and the people of Israel, were gathered together, For to do whatsoever thy hand and thy counsel determined before to be done. And now, Lord behold their threatenings: and grant unto thy servants, that with all boldness they may speak thy word, By stretching forth thine hand to heal; and that signs and wonders may be done by the name of thy holy Child Jesus. And when they had prayed, the place was shaken where they were assembled together, and they were all filled with the Holy Ghost, and they spake the word of God with boldness."* Based on the scriptures, the unadulterated word of God, I can state unequivocally that the Lord Jesus Christ is the Son of God. He is God manifest in the flesh. Anyone who comes with a different revelation is either ignorant, or is a liar.

The Apostle John declared, *"In Jesus Christ there is life and that life was the light of men."* With that revelation in mind, you do not have to be a rocket scientist to understand that, without Jesus, a man is dead spiritually and if he is dead spiritually he is groping around in darkness. Light dispels darkness and knowledge of who Jesus is, not only gives us salvation, it gives us revelation and understanding. Jesus is the light that shines in the darkness but the darkness cannot comprehend Him. John uses the Greek word katalambano for comprehend. It means *to take eagerly, to seize, to possess, and to apprehend.* It comes from the word *kata* which means about, among, and the word *lambano* which means, *to get hold of, to catch.* Unless God the Father opens up the eyes of an individual's understanding, he will never be able to lay hold of or attain the light. An individual can have multiple degrees from the finest institutions, they can attain more wealth than they can spend in their lifetime, they can have the genius that allows them to come up with the greatest ideas, but if they do not have the Son of God they do not have life.

There are many people who have good natural vision but are blind and deceived spiritually. Men would rather believe a lie than the truth. The gospel is the light that can break the power of darkness off the minds of people but they refuse to heed to it. Paul told the Corinthians, *"But if our gospel be hid, it is hid to them that are lost: in whom the god of this world hath blinded the minds of them which believe not, lest the light of the glorious gospel of Christ, who is the image of God, should shine unto them" (2 Corinthians 4:3-4).* The word blinded comes from the Greek word tuphlos (pronounced toof-los); it means physical or mental blindness. Satan is the god of this world's system. He used to be Lucifer the son of the morning until pride was found in him and he was cast down from his lofty position as the covering cherub. He has perverted things and deceived men into thinking that their dark deeds are ok.

In describing the condemnation that would come upon men for rejecting the gift of eternal life, Jesus said, *"And this is the condemnation, that light is come into the world, and men loved darkness rather than light, because their deeds were evil. For everyone that doeth evil hateth the light, neither cometh to the light, lest his deeds should be reproved (John 3:19-20).* The Greek word for deeds is *ergon* and it means to *toil,* to *labor,* and to *work.* Sin is pleasurable because if it was not people would not indulge in it. That is why Jesus declared *"men loved darkness but hate the light."* The light exposes darkness so men hide and salivate on pornographic pictures, they hide and indulge in sexual perversion, they hide and commit all manner of lascivious and licentious acts. The word of God is the light that exposes the hidden sin in our lives and that is why it is difficult for men to sit under a word that comes to them like a two edge sword, especially when they have no desire to have the carnal fleshly nature cut. It is easy to listen to messages that tell us how much we are going to prosper and be blessed. The flesh is challenged when messages are preached that warn us to flee fornication, adultery and other forms of sin. When Jesus said men refused to come to the light so their deeds can be reproved, the Greek word for reproved is *elegcho*; it means to *admonish*, to *convict,* to *convince*, to *rebuke*, and to *tell a fault.* This is the reason why we have to receive a balanced word. If we are going to walk in perfection and maturity, then we have to embrace the whole counsel of God, not just the words that speak of blessings. It is not popular for preachers to use their platform on television and radio to address the sin that is in the world and in the church but it is necessary because only the light of God's word can dispel the darkness. Why do you think you do not hear such messages emanating from your favorite Christian radio and television programs? It is because those types of messages will not get the preacher big offerings, and win him any popularity contests. We must never forget the fact that preaching is not only profitable for doctrine but for correction and reproof so that people can repent and have their transgressions blotted out when the time of refreshing comes.

I am not advocating that preachers beat people over the head with words of condemnation all the time; I am saying we have to teach the whole Bible. The Bible and the Bible alone contain the words of eternal life. It is an absolute correct statement that God desires to prosper and bless His people, but so is the word that says, "Depart from me you workers of iniquity for I knew you not."

When Jesus left His home town of Nazareth and dwelt in Capernaum which is upon the sea coast in the borders of Zabulon and Nephthalim, He did not go vacationing on the beaches of a seaside resort. It was the fulfillment of the prophecy spoken by the prophet Isaiah. *"The land of Zabulon, and the land of Nephthalim, by the way of the sea, beyond Jordan, Galilee of the Gentiles; The people which sat in darkness saw great light; and to them which sat in the region and shadow of death light is sprung up" (Matthew 4:15-16).* Jesus has made us ambassadors and called us "the light of the world" because He expects us to go to places where people are sitting in darkness and the shadow of death so the light of the glorious gospel can shine. Our churches have become so posh, cushy, and pristine that no one wants to leave to go into the highways and the hedges to compel people to come to Jesus. Modern day church buildings show the trappings of wealth and have something for everybody. The sinner can come in and hear a message that makes his flesh feel good but does not convict him of his sin. 1 John 3:8 says, *"He that committeth sin is of the devil; for the devil sinneth from the beginning. For this purpose the Son of God was manifested, that he might destroy the works of the devil."* The works of the devil are manifested in the dark deeds of men.

When a sinner hears the word of God, is convicted, repents of His sin, and asks Jesus into his life, the kingdom of darkness suffers loss. This is why it is imperative for the body of Christ to be about the Lord's business. His business is the preaching of the gospel of the kingdom of God, and making disciples of those who have been converted through the teaching of the Word.

It is interesting to note that after bringing the light to Galilee of the Gentiles Matthew says, "from that time Jesus began to **preach**, and to **say**, "**Repent**: for the kingdom of heaven is at hand." Jesus did not give the people glowing prophecies about prosperity, instead He called them to turn from the darkness of their world to the light of the kingdom. Jesus did not stand up like a motivational speaker attempting to motivate the people to get all they can. The Greek word for preach is kerusso and it means *to herald as a public or town crier*, especially divine truth. It also means to proclaim, or to publish. When an individual is oblivious to some impending danger coming their way, we have to herald or throw something at them to get their attention in order to save their lives. Many people in the earth are going down a slippery dark slope, a precipice of sin and destruction. They need a town crier who is willing to herald the word, *"repent for the kingdom of God is at Hand."* It is a tragedy for an individual to die in the darkness of their sin when they can have access to the light and the life of Jesus Christ. When people sitting in the church refuse to go out and proclaim the gospel; Jesus will raise up ex drug dealers, prostitutes, adulterers, fornicators and others who have been freed from sin. He will use them because they understand that to whom much is given much is required.

As gross darkness covers the earth, as the hearts of men begin to wax cold, the disciples of Jesus Christ must be willing to endure attacks and criticism in-order to herald the gospel. Once the sinner repents and comes to knowledge of the Lordship of Jesus we can teach them the word of God. The Greek word for teach is *didasko* and it means to instruct in doctrine. It has the connotation of using the word of God to bring someone from the place of infancy to a mature adult. It is only the blood of Jesus that can cleanse a person of sin; it is only the light of the glorious gospel of Jesus Christ that can teach that person how to live as a new creature or new species. When a person is trapped in darkness, and all people are trapped in darkness until they are liberated by the saving knowledge of Jesus Christ, no amount of good works can bring transformation, only the light of the gospel can do it.

The Apostle Paul said we have been given the ministry of reconciliation because God was in Christ reconciling the world unto Him. God has not only given us the ministry of reconciliation, He has given us the word of reconciliation. I know we have many ministries in the local church such as, youth ministry, women's ministry, singles ministry, marriage ministry, and so on. Those ministries have their place, but the ministry of reconciliation must never take a back seat to any of those, because those are man made. The ministry of reconciliation was given to the church by Jesus Christ. The Greek word for reconciliation is *katallage* and it means *restoration to divine favor*, or *atonement*. When an individual is truly restored to divine order, society will have better marriages, young people, husbands, fathers and so on. Despite having so many marriage ministries, the divorce rate in the church exceeds that of the world at the present time. We have state of the art youth ministries, but our young people are staying away from church. We have many doctors in the body but few people are being healed. We need to preach the apostolic doctrine of the Lord Jesus Christ and we will witness the restoration of people to God's divine order.

THE FATHER OF LIGHTS

On page 85 of his book, *The Character of God*, R. C. Sproul wrote, "God's shadow never moves. It never moves because He has no shadow. God dwells in blazing light. His very being is the fullness of light. His glory is radiant. Even the sun that floods our planet with light has dark spots. There are no spots on God-no hint of a blemish." As the Apostle James declares: "Every good gift and every perfect gift is from above, and comes down from the Father of lights, with whom there is no variation or shadow of turning" (Jas 1:17). The greatest and most perfect gift any individual can receive from the Father of lights is Jesus Christ. He is the perfect expression of God's love for a lost and dying world. We cannot earn the salvation He brings with any type of religious meritorious works. The only thing required of us is that we receive the Gift of God that is Jesus Christ. This gives me a great segue for one of my favorite passages of scripture; a passage that I believe is the key to all other passages. *"For God so loved the world that he gave his only begotten Son, that whosoever believeth in him should not perish, but have everlasting life. For God sent not his Son into the world to condemn the world; but that the world through him might saved"* (John 3:16-17).

There is absolutely no way to compute the value of Jesus' death on the cross for the sins of the world. All the currency, the gems, pearls and diamonds on the planet would be insufficient to pay the debt Jesus paid. Man's wealth can purchase the toys and the material things that please his flesh but he cannot do anything to gain or earn salvation. Salvation comes by faith alone in Christ alone. Thank God for giving Jesus to us as a gift. There is no reason why anyone in this world should walk in condemnation when the gift of eternal life can be attained through Jesus Christ. The devil will try to make us believe that we are condemned because of our sinful thoughts and actions but we must remember he is a liar and the father of lies. God has given us a precious gift in His Son Jesus and He is able to deliver us from all condemnation. You are one prayer away from deliverance. Please do not believe the lie of the devil. God loved you enough to send Jesus to die in your place so receive your deliverance today. Do not allow the devil to deceive you with false religions and with false gods. Men create their own gods who will allow them to appease their flesh.

Jesus is the true light and anyone who does not understand this is living in deception. Satan can give a false light that causes men to be deceived. *"And no marvel; for Satan himself is transformed into an angel of light. Therefore it is no great thing if his ministers also be transformed as the ministers of righteousness; whose end shall be according to their works" (2 Corinthians 11:14-15).* The Greek word for transformed as it is used here is different from the Greek word used for transformed in *Romans 12:2.* When he told the church at Rome not to be conformed to this world but to be transformed by the renewing of their mind, Paul used the Greek word metamorphoo for transformed; it means to change, or to transfigure. It is the same word used in Matthew 17:2 and Mark 9:2 to describe the transfiguration of Jesus when he took Peter James and John up the mount. The word Paul uses for transformed in *2 Corinthians 11:14-15* is *metaschematizo.* It means to disguise ones self. The light of the glorious gospel of Jesus Christ transforms and changes the life of the believer, it allows him to look, and act and shine like a child of God. The transformation which Satan brings is one that makes dark things look like the light, but there is no change. A person that is in disguise is a person who seeks to keep their identity hidden. Satan is an illusionist, and a master counterfeiter. He disguises himself because if people were able to see him as he really is, they would turn from the darkness of deception and embrace the light of the gospel. He has the uncanny ability to disguise himself as whatever size, shape, color or fragrance that stimulates us. On the surface he will make the thing we desire appealing to our flesh, while hiding the poison which lay beneath the surface.

For the wife who is getting up in age and has body parts that are heading south, he will bring a younger version across the path of the husband. He will convince the deceived husband that he will be better off with a younger woman. When the husband leaves his wife of many years for the younger more voluptuous female, he has to wine, dine, and practically spend every dime to keep her. The devil knows the packages that stimulate our senses and if we allow any opening he will make sure the package is delivered. What about the young female who allows a slick, smooth, talking young man or even an older man to whisper sweet things into her ears? Her emotions cause her to throw caution to the wind by disregarding the words of her guardians. As soon as the man gets what he wants he is on to the next gullible, unsuspecting victim. On many occasions the female is left pregnant and has to fend for herself. The sad part of the whole situation is the fact that a great deal of the responsibility for caring for her when she is pregnant and after she gives birth falls on the same guardian(s) who warned her not to get involved with the snake in the first place.

The reason why momma, grandmamma, and aunty can warn you about the slippery two legged snake is, they have been beguiled and fell victim to some of them in their younger days. The devil does not have new tricks; he has new people to trick. The clothing, the cologne, the mode of transportation and the speech may have changed but it is still the same old devil, imp, pimp, and demon, disguising themselves as messengers of light. If he does not want to work now, he is not going to want to work after you say "I do." If he does not treat you with respect now, what makes you think he will, once the honeymoon is over? If he is hooked on porn at the present time, he will not be miraculously delivered by matrimony. He will expect you to position yourself and act out some of the images he sees the porn ladies acting out. Many people have been blinded and beguiled by the charm and the charisma of the snake's cool slick persona, only to wake up in darkness with AIDS, Herpes, Syphilis, Gonorrhea or some other sexually transmitted disease.

The brother might look and sound like a real man but many of them are on the down low these days. Once upon a time some men used to have a woman on the side, but things have gotten so perverse that some men have another man on the side. If you do not have discernment you better get caller ID. You better do a fruit check because you might be sleeping with the enemy.

Satan sends out probes to see if there are any openings. Once he spots one he will send a particular spirit to attack us in that area. We must allow the word of the Lord to fill the chambers of our souls so there will be no room for the adversary to operate. Jesus said, *"For the prince of this world cometh, and hath nothing in me" (John 14:30).*

It is not a matter of if but when the prince of this world will come at us with some sin laden enticements. We have to make sure there is no room or place in us for him or his minions to operate. We have to fill the chambers of our souls with prayer, worship and meditation on the word. We cannot spend hours watching our favorite television programs that entertain our flesh, and expect to be victorious when the tempter comes. The part of us we feed is the part that will gain strength. When the tempter came to Jesus in the wilderness he came when Jesus was hungry and began to tempt Him by telling Him to turn stones into bread. Jesus responded by telling him, *"It is written, Man shall not live by bread alone, but by every word that proceedeth out of the mouth of God" (Matthew 4: 4).* Bread represents those things which sustain our physical bodies. God knows that bread is necessary but every word that proceeds out of the mouth of God is essential, for physical as well as spiritual growth. In each phase of being tempted by the devil, Jesus told him what was written; when the devil could not get Jesus to fall he departed. Some translations say he left for a more seasonable or opportune time. We can be sure the devil is always looking for the right moment to send something or someone across our path to entice us. He is a crafty being so he will not show the destruction that is behind the scenes. His desire is to get the individual to take the bait so he can put a hook in them.

Satan is not coming as a hideous creature with pointed ears, a tail and a pitchfork. He is able to disguise himself as an angel of light. That was the disguise he used when he deceived Eve. The creature that conversed with Eve in the garden is called a serpent. The Hebrew word for serpent is *"nachash"* and it means, *"The shining one."* many women have been deceived by men they thought were the ideal husband because the person dressed nice, smelled good, had some money and was articulate. Not long after the honeymoon they realized they married a two legged serpent, a devil. Be careful who you are groping, or rolling in the hay with at night. The honeymoon does not last forever. Was it not Jacob who thought he had Rachel, but when the light of the morning began to shine he realized he had married tender-eyed Leah? Enjoy your singleness and use your discernment when dating. Do not allow the loneliness of your flesh to lead you into unholy matrimony. Many people are in marriages that have caused years of torment; the amazing thing is some have married serpents on several different occasions. "Once bitten, twice shy," the old adage goes. You would think after being bitten once, a man or woman would do their due diligence before saying "I do." Some people appear to have a high threshold for pain. The serpent will say "I do" to get what he wants, and then he will say "I won't and I don't."

THE OMNIPOTENT CREATOR

On page 121 of his book *The Character Of God* Dr. R. C. Sproul shared a great story that gives great insight into the Omnipotence of God the creator of the heavens and the Earth. Dr. Sproul wrote, "I sat in terrified silence the first day of my freshman class in astronomy. The professor posed a question for us: "suppose that we have a scale wherein an inch equals a million miles. How far would it be to the nearest star apart from our sun? Would it be one hundred feet? Three hundred feet? Or five hundred feet?

My mind began to calculate frantically. Twelve inches make one foot. One foot then would mean twelve million miles. Multiply that by one hundred and the first option meant a distance of over a billion miles. Now, I knew that our sun was ninety-three million miles from the earth. It seemed reasonable that the next nearest star would not be much more than ten times that distance, so I guessed one hundred feet was the correct answer. I was wrong. So were all the other students who guessed either three hundred feet or five hundred feet. The professor fooled us. He said, "None of the above." He went on to explain that the nearest star was approximately the distance from Pittsburgh to Chicago with each inch equaling a million miles. He gave us a little more help. "Light travels at a rate of 186,000 miles per second. That is, in one second light can travel seven-and-a-half times around the earth. The light that we see twinkling at night from the nearest star left that star on its way to Earth four-and-a-half years ago"(Sproul)!

"The distance from earth to the nearest star is four-and-a-half light years away. Traveling at a speed of 186,000 miles per second it takes over four years to reach us! I could not fathom such immensity. When I left class, I was in a daze. I had mixed feelings" (Sproul).

On the one hand, I was staggered by the apparent insignificance of the planet Earth and of R. C. Sproul. I felt like a speck in a vast universe. Yet, I was also awestruck by the sheer magnitude of power that could make a universe so gigantic as to contain billions of stars in mega billions of distances from each other. My mind snapped back to Genesis 1. Here is the biblical description of God's mighty work of creation: In the beginning God created the heavens and the earth. The earth was without form, and void; and darkness was on the face of the deep. And the Spirit of God was hovering over the face of the waters. Then God said, "Let there be light"; and there was light. Genesis 1:1-3

The last line, "and there was light", is totally mystifying! God spoke. He commanded light to come into existence. Light began to shine. This is what Saint Augustine called the Divine Imperative. The world was created by the sheer power of God's voice.

In the same manner that the Spirit of God hovered over the face of the waters when darkness was on the face of the deep, God the Holy Spirit is hovering over your midnight situation, waiting for the Lord to speak the words, *"let there be light."* When the Almighty Omnipotent creator commands the light to shine, darkness must give way. The mortal mind can not comprehend or fully fathom the power and majesty of the Almighty God. Without the indwelling of the Holy Ghost, the mind can not understand the fact that God did all the creating through the pre-incarnate Christ. He allowed the Word to become flesh and to tabernacle among us. He did it because He loves us with an everlasting love and wants us to dwell eternally in His presence. In His presence there is fullness of joy and at His right hand there are pleasures evermore. The thing that is absolutely mind boggling is what Jesus went through to allow us to dwell in the presence of the Father of lights. He was wounded for our transgressions and bruised for our iniquities according to the Prophet Isaiah. He was spat upon, forced to wear a crown of thorns, nailed to a cross to suffer a painful agonizing death. In light of what Jesus went through for us, do you understand why you have to persevere through your midnight, by carrying your cross? The Apostle Paul told the church at Rome, *"For*

I reckon that the sufferings of this present time are not worthy to be compared with the glory which shall be revealed in us" (Romans 8:18).

Your midnight hour will take you to the breaking point at times, but remember it can not be compared to the glory which will be revealed in you. The greater the suffering the greater the glory; Jesus was able to ask His Father to give Him the glory that he had with Him from the beginning. He deserved this, because he endured the cross and despised the shame. He went through the greatest time of suffering any individual could because He took upon himself the sins of the world. Can you imagine the sins of the world being laid on one person? My God!!!

Do you understand why Jesus is "the way the truth and the life." Do you understand why "no man cometh to the Father but by Him." Do you understand why "there is no other name given under heaven by which a man can be saved?" Buddhism can give a certain amount of enlightenment but Jesus is the true light. A Buddhist can meditate and levitate into the air but when he comes down his soul will still be darkened by a carnal nature. Jesus is the only one who can command the light to shine out of a dark soul. Islam, and Hinduism have facets of truth but Jesus is the Truth. There is a difference between something that has some truth and something that is the truth. Jesus is truth personified.

He is the light that God shined in our dark hearts and provided salvation for us. Our midnight experiences will not destroy us, but will help us to die daily so we can get to the place where the light of His glory is shining and radiating in and through us. The thesis and the central point in this book is, do not allow the darkness of your current circumstance to lead you into a dark place of despair. Allow God's precious light to shine in that dark place. Let prayer and praise be the keys that unlock the door to deliverance. It is Midnight let us give God praise.

Testimonies of Deliverance

Pastor Samuel N Greene

Years ago I went through a very trying midnight experience. My precious wife had taken our children to see her parents which left me, a very busy Pastor, home alone. As I was beginning this time, having just completed a glorious set of meetings, I was looking forward to just beginning my first day off in quite a long time. One of the first things I did was go to the mailbox to get my mail, and within that mail was a package from a friend. I opened it only to find this person sent me a picture of someone from my past.

It brought back many painful, horrible moments of one of the most trying times in my life. Now before I opened this letter, I had been in a time of great worship with the Lord. I was in an anointed and blessed place. But as I read this letter and saw this picture, suddenly I was overcome with grief, regret, and great sorrow. I immediately became deeply depressed, so much so that I despaired of life. Darkness descended upon me with such an overwhelming cloud. The more I meditated and thought about this horrible time of suffering, it got worse and worse, so much so, that I was overcome by a great heaviness.

Demonic voices began to invade my home and my own soul. It only took seconds for thoughts of suicide and deep, deep regret to permeate my mind. I just could not see any reason for going on. As this continued this horrible storm of darkness, regret, condemnation, and depression descended upon me. I went back to my bedroom and fell upon my bed. As I did, the darkness and overwhelming cloud of condemnation grew stronger and stronger. I could hardly breathe. I can barely describe to you how great the darkness was which filled me and my house. But suddenly, deep, deep down inside of me, I heard a still small voice telling me to begin to praise the Lord Jesus. I could barely hear it, and nothing in me wanted to praise God. Thank God for the Holy Ghost, for He would not leave me alone.

So I began to try to speak and praise God. It was extremely difficult because the devils were taunting me. But I persisted and the more I sang and praised Jesus, light began to come into my tortured soul. Then, as I got bolder and bolder, the Glory of God descended upon me. God literally and came down to help me from the heavens. Little by little, moment by moment, God's Holy, enveloping Glory began to rise in me and then through my home. Light so bright drove the demons, the depression, regret, and the darkness away until there was no darkness at all in me or my house. Jesus then spoke to me and said "you have now overcome this thing and it will never bother you again." He told me I had conquered it completely by simply doing what I had preached to others thousands of times before. Now I had the authority over it. By God's grace and persistence I passed through the midnight hour and I learned a tremendous lesson. Jesus will never leave us or forsake us, and there is no situation or circumstance that is so dark or horrible that He can not overcome.

Pastor Samuel N Greene

Marcia's Midnight

My midnight experience came in 2006 when I entered into a business transaction with an individual who turned out to be a wolf in sheep's clothing. When I met him he presented himself as a man of God of good character, integrity, and sound business principles. I invested a large sum of money in the business over a period of time, based on how he presented himself and how he presented the business opportunity.

All that glitters is not gold so we have to exercise discernment and sound judgment with every association. The transaction failed due to his greed, self reliance, pride and poor managerial decisions. When it failed, he abused me emotionally and mentally which caused me to sink into a state of deep depression. I was in a dark and desperate place. I shared my distress with some of the people in my local church and they kicked me to the curb. One of my friends overheard one of the church members in a discussion with another church member. They accused me of sleeping with the man, and figured that was the reason why I invested a large sum of money with him. I must admit that the most dangerous folks to hurt anyone are church folks. We have an expectation that we can receive solace and comfort from people in the church when we a going through a difficult period. The treatment I received from some of the people in my local church caused me to become very paranoid and more depressed.

I would like to share with you some of the experiences of my depression. I suffered a total loss of interest in everything I once enjoyed. I went to bed very early at nights and stayed there until the next afternoon. I took tablets to sleep and tablets to keep awake when I had to go to work. I got up everyday and felt like I had no purpose and nothing productive to accomplish. Eventually, I took a leave of absence from work. I had more time, but no purpose. I became a recluse, because I did not have a desire to socialize with anyone. I became so fearful of getting out of bed that I limited the amounts of liquid I took so I would not have to go to the bathroom. Bathing was a great chore because it took too much energy and I was already functioning on minimal energy. I slept on the carpet in my narrow closet for months. I laid there curled up in the fetal position, in the dark, because being in the dark gave me a sense of security.

Occasionally I still attended my local church. I was crying out for help with a pitch which was undetected by those surrounding me. It is possible to be in a crowd, yet suffer severe loneliness, and the mental torture of deep depression. I could not pray, I could not cry, and I could not find anything to praise God for. During my darkest hours there were precious saints travailing in prayer and fasting before God for me. My precious aunt in Jamaica was one of the people who prayed without ceasing for me. One of my close friends, a church sister and a prayer warrior, came to the house and told me she was determined not to lose me to suicide. During that period my godmother took me to a service where Brother Fidel Donaldson was ministering. He prayed for me and ministered the word of the Lord to me. The prayer and the ministry of the word started the process of my deliverance.

Suddenly, one morning in 2009, I was awakened at about 4am with the song *"The Comforter Has Come." The line which JUMPED out at and ministered to my spirit was, "The long, long night has passed, the morning breaks at last, and hushed the dreadful wail and fury of the blast, as over the golden hills the day advances fast, the comforter has come."* There was another verse of the song which also spoke to my spirit, and it says, "Lo, the great King of kings with healing in His wings, to every captive soul a full deliverance brings; and through the vacant cells a song of triumph rings: the Comforter has come. When the Comforter came He took away the need for tablets to sleep and also to stay awake. I have continued to walk in my deliverance ever since.

Oh boundless love divine, how shall this tongue of mine, to wandering mortal tell the matchless grace divine?

The man who was instrumental in my depression came under serious judgment by the hand of God. Many people told me that I should have had him arrested, but I left his judgment to God. His vehicle was repossessed. He was evicted several times, and he had to live in a shelter. He was taken to court for child support. He had to go on disability and had to live on food stamps. His driver's license was suspended. He lost most of his possessions. He was reduced to being a vagabond. He has not been able to find a job for over one year, in spite of all his educational qualifications, and his standing in the local church. He was marketing director of Sprint for several years. He is a teacher by profession, the choir director and a counselor at the church he attended. He had the nerve to call me one day to say that he was hungry and needed money to buy food.

His deceptive actions resulted in my midnight experience, but my deliverance came through the word of God, intercessory prayer, fasting and the song of the Lord. If you are presently experiencing a midnight crisis, please be encouraged, and know that the Comforter remains the same yesterday, today, and forever; He is an ever present help in the time of trouble.

Marcia Orlebar

Martin's Midnight

My midnight began in March 1984. I was getting dressed for school when I noticed a lump on the right side of my neck. My initial reaction was that it was just a swelling or even mumps. My siblings had already left for work so I told my girlfriend and we agreed that I should go to the doctor. The next day I went to the doctor's office in the neighborhood. Doctor Abraham was an older gentleman in his late fifties about average height. I was not particularly nervous as I sat in the waiting room because I didn't feel it was anything major. I was called to take an x-ray, and sent back to the waiting room when it was completed. My frame of mind as I waited was still relatively calm. Finally after waiting about 30 minutes, I was called into Doctor Abraham's office. He informed me that I had cancer. Yes, the dreaded C word. It is the diagnosis no one wants to receive. Thank God, I had recently accepted the Lord Jesus as my personal savor. God's timing is perfect. He knew what I had to face before I did. He knew I would not be able to rely on my own strength. He knew I would need the strength of Jesus to make through.

I was scared, shocked, and had feelings of sorry and confusion. I went back home and fell into a state of deep depression. I could not imagine how I could have gotten cancer. We hear about others getting the dreaded disease but never think it will happen to us. My mind raced with thoughts of how it could have happened to me. I had been eating properly and taking vitamins and minerals. I ran two to three miles at least once a week. I lifted weights three times a week, and I was not a smoker; but there I was with cancer? In my mind I was the least likely candidate.

I asked the LORD, why me? I told my family and they were very encouraging, but I knew they were gravely concerned. I knew the lump did not appear over night, but I could not remember ever seeing it before. I sat in my room and cried. It was midnight in every sense of the word. My mother could not handle the news so she called my brother. My brother suggested that I visit a doctor in Connecticut in-order to get a second opinion. Doctor Abraham had told me to get a second opinion. My girlfriend told me not to go to Connecticut, but to believe GOD for healing. I was scared so I went. I was a young Christian and the cancer diagnosis was a test of my faith.

I saw the doctor in Connecticut and he confirmed Dr. Abraham's diagnosis. I was admitted to the hospital immediately and was subjected to a battery of tests. The nurses took four vials of blood from me, once in the day, and once in the night. I never knew I had that much blood in me. A group of doctors and interns came around to examine me and to speak with me. In examining me, they squeezed the lump on my neck. I felt no pain at first, but after three or four days, my neck was very sore. After a while, I stopped them from squeezing my neck because the pain was excruciating. My midnight was exacerbated when another lump about the size of fifty cent piece was found on my chest, right below my collarbone. The new discovery meant the cancer had spread.

I was told by the team of doctors that I needed to have a biopsy done on the second lump because it was more accessible. The nurse came in and gave me a drip. I could not eat that day and became very drowsy. When the time for the operation drew near, I was wheeled into the operating room, given some anesthesia, and told to count backwards. I woke up in the recovery room a couple hours later. Thank God, I felt no pain. The doctors told me they were concerned because I took along time to wake up. I was sent back to my room after I recovered. When I got back to my room, there was an older black man in his sixties who had a bed next to me. They brought him in while I was being prepared for surgery. It did not take me long to find out that he had some mental issues. He repeatedly spoke to the walls and the ceiling. He kept asking me if I saw the spirits that were in the room. Needless to say, I prayed.

Some of the tests I had taken were CAT scan, bone biopsy, tissue biopsy, Gallium Scan and x-rays.

When it was time to have the bone biopsy I was given a local anesthetic near my pelvic bone. I was told to lie on my stomach. I could not see what was happening but I was about to feel it. They stuck an instrument through my skin into my pelvic bone in-order to extract bone and marrow. The pain was indescribable. I shrieked as the pain reverberated through every fiber of my being. Whoever said men should not cry, never felt pain like that. I screamed in horror and bit the pillow. As they pulled the instrument out of my body, I could feel tissue coming out with it.

Another test I had was the Gallium scan. That test was administered to detect whether or not the cancer had spread to other parts of my body. I had to lie on back while both of my feet were injected with a dye. The dye traveled throughout my body and an additional scan was given to check other areas of my body for cancer. The nurse gave me some local anesthesia for my feet. I had no idea what was going on. I remember feeling liquid trickling down my feet. Once the test was over I noticed they sutured my feet. I was very surprised because I had no idea that they were going to cut both of my feet. The liquid I felt trickling down my feet was blood.

After a whole week of tests, I was diagnosed with stage 2E Hodgkin's disease, which is cancer of the lymph nodes. The lymph nodes are where the white blood cells are made for the body's defense. I was told I had a lump the size of an orange in my chest, between my lungs, another spot near my liver, and another on the base of my neck. I could not sleep on my stomach as I had done for so many years. The pain was continual because the cancer kept growing. I remember when I was in high school in Trinidad. There were times when I experienced pain in my chest, and playing doctor, I said to myself, it is probably gas pain. But in all the physical pain, and the trials, the LORD was with me. I felt HIS presence in the hospital room. He ministered to me as I ministered to HIM. My faith was strengthened by His presence and I could feel the fear lift off of me. I read the word constantly, and prayed without ceasing.

After a week of tests they sent me home. I was told I must start Chemotherapy as soon as possible because by July the pain was getting worse. A family acquaintance got me in Memorial Sloan Kettering to see the doctors. They agreed that I should start treatment as soon as possible. The treatment they suggested was four cycles' of chemotherapy and one cycle of radiation. I had to quit college because chemo and radiation would have me very sick. I had to stop exercising because all cells in my body would be destroyed by the chemo and radiation. I was given a large amount of documents to sing. After signing the documents I was reminded by the doctor that I should have some of my sperm store in a sperm bank if I planned on having children in the future because the Chemo and Radiation would kill the good cells as well as the bad ones. I was not married at the time and made a decision not to masturbate or sleep with a woman.

When the day came to get my first treatment, my mother was with me. I could not travel by myself after I got the treatment because of nausea and dizziness. It was about two o'clock and the waiting room was filled with a lot of patients. The room had the feeling of sickness and death in the atmosphere. A nurse called my name and was put into another room the nurse asked me a hundred questions, did I smoke, did I drink, was I a painter, was I exposed to chemicals and pesticides. Another nurse took all my vitals and I was ushered into the treatment room. The room was filled with patients hooked up to IVs. I was made to sit down and the nurse swabbed my arm. A needle was inserted into my arm and the chemo started. I felt a cold sensation as it traveled into my arm and body. About forty five minutes later I had a metallic dry taste in my mouth and I was finished. I had to travel on a train that rocked back and fort, bumps and turns for an hour feeling sick, nausea and dizzy. I also was concerned about being constipated from the drugs. There were many other side effects but I do not remember them. The train was packed with the rush hour crowd and I feared throwing up. When I finally got home I went straight to bed.

My diet consisted of bland food, broiled chicken, fish or veal, no seasonings or not fried, baked, barbequed or stewed. Each morning I got up and there was hair on my pillow and bed. But the LORD was with me, I felt HIS presence. Everyday I prayed and sang praises to the LORD. There were times when HE sent me out on the streets to witness in the neighborhood. I began to search the scriptures on faith and healing. I mediated on them until they became part of me. I remember I was asked if I was going to a church service where Evangelist was preaching, and I said no because I was not feeling well.

She said to me that I should press my way that the LORD will bless me. I went praising GOD despite how I felt. While she was speaking in the service she spoke a word of knowledge saying that there was someone here who has a stomach ulcer and if they praise GOD, HE will heal them. I did not know I had an ulcer but I praised HIM anyway. I always got a pain in my stomach when I ate something but I did not know what caused it. A few days later I did not get any pains in my stomach and the LORD reminded me of that moment in the service. I went to services every time the doors were opened. I went to spring, summer and back to school revivals seeking for the HOLY SPIRIT. In the month of August the LORD filled me with HIS HOLY SPIRIT.

As time went on I was loosing hair as my body absorbed the chemo. My white blood cell count dropped dramatically. They were so low at times that they doctors warned me to stay away from anyone who was sick. I could not catch a cold, flu, virus or any disease because my defense system was weak. I did not spend a lot of time at home but I went to the parks, museums anything to get my mind of my sickness. My nails on my fingers and my veins in my arms were dark because of the chemo. After every two or three weeks of chemo and I would get a week break from it. I remember taking pills to counteract the chemo and it made me loose sleep. I did not sleep at all the previous night and the second night I was struggling to fall asleep, it was about 3:30 am I got so frustrated I prayed and GOD faithfully answered I fell asleep at 4 am. Another time I had taken chemo couple of days before, I was at my girlfriend's house and my tongue came out of my mouth, I had no control, I could not pull it back in or move it side to side. Her family thought I was having a seizure so they rushed me to a near by hospital. I was taken to emergency and was put in for observation. When I laid down on a gurney, I regained control of my tongue but the doctor felt that I should stay in emergency for an hour. When the hour came the doctor gave us the okay to leave but the HOLY SPIRIT said to me it is not over. As we got near to door my tongue came out of my mouth once more. We stayed another hour until they released me, GOD is so awesome. The following week I saw my doctor at Memorial Sloan Kettering and he told me oh it was just a side effect. I wanted to choke the doctor because he was so casual about it. One day it was time for the chemo but my sister could not go because she was busy at work. I was so sad that day but as I got off the train to change trains GOD sent me an angel. HE was preaching the gospel on the platform. Hearing the gospel that day encouraged me, it brought a smile to my face. I was talking to him and I turned to look at something and as I turned back to him he was gone without trace.

After three cycles of chemo went by the time came for me to begin radiation. The waiting room was filled with children and I was so heart broken to see their faces. They looked hopeless, scared, weak and frail. The radiation machine was huge towering over me. It was intimidating because I did not know what to expect. They marked my body with Indian ink and they began the therapy. The next day clumps of hair were on the bed. I did not have to shave because the chemo and the radiation took care of it but my hair on my scalp was thinning out. The back of my head was bald, forming a horse shoe design. I was so humiliated and people stared at me as I walked by on the streets even at church. People actually thought it was a hair style. I bought a hat and it gave me a little bit of confidence. Jesus feels every bit of our pain, sickness and discomfort, HE is so good. The radiation made me feel nausea but it was not as bad as the chemo.

One day as I was worshiping HIM and enjoying HIS presence, my mother or sister called me and I told me she could not join me to go for chemo. I was sad because I did not want to go to the hospital by myself, the HOLY SPIRIT spoke to me and said HE will heal me and I do not have to go for chemo. I got out of shower rejoicing and called the hospital. They said I should come and take the chemo because the cancer can begin to grow larger. The enemy immediately spoke to me and told me I should go to the hospital. My father called from Trinidad and said it was not a good idea because a neighbor said she trusted GOD to heal her and she died. But the LORD was with me, HE is faithful and true, after ten or twelve years later I went to a doctor and did a cancer screen. The results were no trace of cancer. GOD had healed my body as HE said HE would and my family faith grew!! Halleluiah!!!

Martin Montantine

Tracy's Midnight

I was informed early one evening that an influential connection I was developing was terminated before I could fully see it in operation. A connection in which I knew the Lord had ordained and confirmed. I said," Lord how could this be? I am on the straight and narrow road which leads to eternal life." (Matthew 7:14). He did not answer. So I continued to pray and weep the entire evening. I had wept so much that I felt as if all the fluids in my body were depleted and my face was swollen.

Finally, by the am I had fallen asleep with no answer. I arose once again two hours later. I was totally lethargic and to my surprise it was time for morning service. I did not have a permanent church. However, I did attend a particular church inconsistently. Mostly, at my own convenience. Then He spoke, and instructed me to visit a particular church. I had only been there a few times. He said, "There is a message for you."So I drank a cup of coffee to wake myself up and got dressed. Although I was still exhausted. I was eager to find out what the message was.

As praise and worship ceased the pastor opened his Bible slowly. Seriousness infiltrated the atmosphere. With much anticipation of the message I sat straight up in the chair with perfect posture. My knees and legs perfectly aligned as that of a stenographer in a courtroom. Then he distinctly and slowly pronounced the words, "The title of today's message is THE SPIRIT OF NONCOMPLIANCE. Instantly, I wanted to do a rebel cry. A cry that would sound like the screech of a chalkboard when a person drags their fingernails across it. A cry that would cause a sound proof glass window to come crashing down. The tears came down my face but I refused to make the sound. My body went limp, my mind chaotic." I might as well have been flat like a piece of paper that when dropped down on the floor lightly slides underneath the chair in front of you. "How Lord? How could you be saying this to me? I have done the best I could do in ministry." I am not committing adultery, lying, stealing and murdering. He quickly reminded me about the many times he would whisper, "Get ready for church." I would reply, "In just a moment," then fall back to sleep. Just to wake up later and go to my beautiful riverfront lanai the Lord had just blessed me with to read my Bible there. Also, the time he wanted me to go on certain trips the ministry was involved in and I had an excuse for most of them. When reminded of this and more I had not really been compliant (obedient) to the spirit of God at all. I began to repent so much aloud by the time the service was over I was empty of the SPIRIT OF NONCOMPLIANCE. Hallelujah! MY MIDNIGHT had finally taken place. Unshackled by the delusion of righteousness. A RELIGIOUS TOOL of Satan. I never like to capitalize satan's name. LOL! Getting back to the subject at hand.

What we must understand is that God loves us so much that He would take the time out to speak to a particular pastor, have you go to a specific church, at an orchestrated date and time to correct you. HOLY! HOLY! HOLY! LORD GOD ALMIGHTY! Suppose that Pastor woke up and decided to preach a different message than what the Lord told him.

Furthermore, what if he had been me when the Lord told him to get up and preach the message. He had responded," Ok first I need a little more sleep." Then he missed church altogether and went outside to preach the message of noncompliance to himself. God needs his people in obedience. Lives are at stake! This is not all about you. It is about your family, neighbors, friends, foes and those in between. You must humble yourself to the total will of God. God will also hide you (as he told me) if you are not ready. Sometimes men and women of God will not recognize you. On the inside you will be asking, why are they passing me over. Trust the God in them. Even God will not unveil you to them until the appointed time.

The bible clearly warns "There is a way that seems right to man but the end thereof are the ways of death" (Proverbs. 14:12). He also states, "Wide is the gate and broad is the way that leads to destruction and many there be which go in" (Matt 7:13). God can ordain something but when we are disobedient his plans for us shift. At least for us it seems that way. But He is ALPHA and OMEGA. He already knew what you were going to do before you did it. YOU WERE SET UP FOR SUCH A TIME AS THIS. MIDNIGHT!

Tracy Stephens

BIBLIOGRAPHY

Arthur, Kay: The Peace & Power of Knowing God's Name. Colorado Springs, Colorado: WaterBrook Press, 2002

Cunningham, Gene. The basics: A Categorical Bible Study. Bigelow, AR: American Inland Mission, Inc. 1990

Conner, Kevin J. Interpreting The Symbols And Types: Portland, Oregon: City Christian Publishing, 1992

Sproul, R. C. The Character of God: Discovering The God Who Is. Ann Arbor, Michigan: Servant Publications, 1995

Strong, James. The New Strongs Exhaustive Concordance of The Bible. Nashville: Thomas Nelson, Inc. 1995

CPSIA information can be obtained
at www.ICGtesting.com
Printed in the USA
JSHW031022060721
16610JS00001B/67